What Would Sipowicz Do?

EDITED BY GLENN YEFFETH

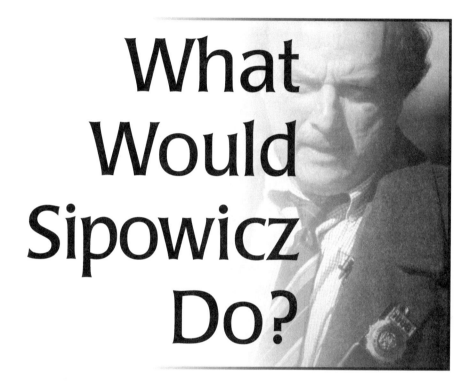

What Would Sipowicz Do?

Race, Rights and Redemption in
NYPD Blue

BENBELLA

BENBELLA BOOKS
Dallas, Texas

"From Sisyphus to Junior" © 2004 by Steven Rubio
"Saving Society One Broken Home at a Time" © 2004 by Joyce Millman
"Watching Jill and Diane" © 2004 by Sharon Bowers
"'English, Doc, English'" © 2004 by Jennifer Parks
"Interrogating Guilty Suspects" © 2004 by George C. Thomas III and Richard A. Leo
"Racism and Reality in *NYPD Blue*" © 2004 by Kenneth Meeks
"Fancy Footwork" © 2004 by Maurice Broaddus
"Just One Sip for Sipowicz to Slip" © 2004 by Jeffrey Schaler
"In Search of Blanche Dubois" © 2004 by David Gerrold
"Forensic Linguistics in *NYPD Blue*" © 2004 by Robert Leonard
"Sipowicz's Progress" © 2004 by Maurice Broaddus
"What Would the *Blue* Do?" © 2004 by David Bruce
"Bare Butts, Bare Souls" © 2004 by Ellen Kirschman
"Fearless Femmes or Wanton Women?" © 2004 by Joy Davidson
"Darwin and Sipowicz" © 2004 by Glenn Yeffeth
"Extra Points for Strippers" © 2004 by Roxanne Conrad

Additional materials © 2004 BenBella Books

BenBella Books, 6440 N. Central Expressway, Suite 617, Dallas, TX 75206

Publisher: Glenn Yeffeth
Editor: Shanna Caughey
Associate Editor: Leah Wilson
Director of Marketing/PR: Laura Watkins

Send feedback to feedback@benbellabooks.com

Printed in the United States of America
10 9 8 7 6 5 4 3 2 1

Library of Congress Cataloging-in-Publication Data

What would Sipowicz do? : race, rights, and redemption in nypd blue / edited by Glenn Yeffeth.
    p. cm.
  ISBN 1-932100-34-2
  1. NYPD blue (Television program) I. Yeffeth, Glenn, 1961-
PN1992.77.N96W53 2004
791.45'72--dc22

                                                                                    2004025350

Cover design by Todd Michael Bushman
Text design and composition by John Reinhardt Book Design

Distributed by Independent Publishers Group. To order call (800) 888-4741. www.ipgbook.com
For special sales contact Laura Watkins at laura@benbellabooks.com

Acknowledgments

I'd like to thank Shanna Caughey and Leah Wilson for the hard work they put in editing the essays in this volume. They are, in many ways, the co-editors of this book.

I'd also like to acknowledge Rebecca Green who proofed this book, Todd Bushman who designed the front cover and John Reinhardt who designed the interior. John always does an outstanding job of creating a distinctive but highly readable design and this book is no exception.

To the hardworking detectives of the NYPD and all the others who comprise the thin blue line so the rest of us have the freedom and safety to write books, care for our families and yes, even watch NYPD Blue.

Contents

STEVEN RUBIO

From Sisyphus to Junior, Or How Andy Sipowicz Made *NYPD Blue* Safe for Syndication

Surly, craggy-faced and often unpleasant, Andy Sipowicz seems an unlikely hero. And he wasn't supposed to be. The leading man was supposed to be the melancholy John Kelly, with Sipowicz serving as his troubled and erratic partner. But David Caruso left the show after one season for supposedly greener pastures (we all know how that turned out) and so NYPD Blue was forced to turn to Sipowicz. Somehow it worked out extravagantly well (for eleven more seasons and counting). At least, that's the conventional wisdom. But Rubio has a different interpretation; as he explains, it couldn't have happened any other way.

NYPD BLUE BEGAN IN 1993 as a cop show with an edge. Fans of Steven Bochco's earlier shows may have expected *NYPD Blue*, like *Hill Street Blues* and *L.A. Law*, to be an ensemble drama; the large cast featured no one who would have been considered a star at the time. More than a decade later, though, it is Andy Sipowicz—and the actor who plays him, Dennis Franz—who is the single most recognizable feature of *NYPD Blue*. The only character to have been with the show throughout its long run, Andy has come to represent the program in the popular mind. While other characters come and go, Andy Sipowicz remains, constant in his presence if not in the makeup of his character, which has evolved over time. Although *NYPD Blue* is still nominally an ensemble cop drama, over the years it has become less a show about a group of workmates in the job environment, and more a show about Andy and his partners and fellow cops. This has created a hierarchy of characters, with Andy at the top, his partner as second among equals and everyone else in the cast as supporting players to the two leads.

It was not always this way. In the show's first season, and the first part of the second season, *NYPD Blue* was also a show about one cop, his partners and his workmates, but Andy Sipowicz was the partner in those first episodes; the central character around which the show was based was Det. John Kelly, played by David Caruso. Kelly was a much different character than Sipowicz: if Andy was the Everyman as reformed racist drunk, John Kelly was the existential hero, a contemporary Sisyphus whose worldview was equal parts Albert Camus and Dirty Harry Callahan.

As would be expected, a show centered on Sisyphus was markedly different from the show which emerged after Caruso/Kelly's departure. Andy Sipowicz has worked with many partners since, from Kelly's replacement Bobby Simone to Andy's current partner, John Clark, Jr. While we were told that Andy was John Kelly's mentor, in those first episodes it was clearly Kelly who was taking care of Sipowicz. Since Kelly left, Andy has become the on-screen father figure. Andy Sipowicz has become *NYPD Blue*; *NYPD Blue* has become Andy Sipowicz.

I would argue, in fact, that Andy Sipowicz is the reason *NYPD Blue* has lasted as long as it has. Andy is a complex guy. He has a number of character flaws, as well as many good points—a variety that makes him a useful center for a television series interested in longevity: it takes a long time to exhaust the possibilities in a character with as many built-in features as Andy Sipowicz. If you then consider the interactions between Andy and his various partners, all of whom have their own sets of possibilities, you have an even stronger basis for a long-lasting series. But Andy's complexity is familiar: his possibilities are mostly those that can be found in other standard television series characters. He's a cop, he's a drunk, he's a racist, he's a canny detective, he's a husband, he's a father, he's a partner, he's a mentor.... This is a varied character, but in ordinary ways. To be fair, the excellence of Dennis Franz in the role means even the most simpleminded presentations of Andy are filled with depth. But Franz's acting chops aside, Andy is only complex in the standard television way. This makes him easy to take, over the course of seasons.

None of this is true for Detective Kelly. John Kelly, who on the surface is a simpler character with a more focused set of problems, is in fact a far deeper, more challenging one. Maintaining the depth of Kelly's character would have come at a cost for *NYPD Blue* if he hadn't left the show early on: while Andy's volatile nature can be tamed enough to be tolerable over the long haul while still holding enough edge to be interesting, John Kelly's moody existential angst could never be tamed to a tolerable level without losing its essence.

Especially in the early seasons, Sipowicz battled personal demons. His worldview, like Kelly's and indeed like that of most cops in series television, was informed by the daily grind of dealing with perps and skels, but for Andy such problems took a backseat to his alcoholism, a more personal than social problem (at least as Andy suffered from it). John Kelly's personal problems, on the other hand, grew out of his overall existential suffering: Detective Kelly wanted to save the world, one person at a time, but the effort left him less able to solve the problems of his daily life than he needed to be. When the series began, Andy was a divorced man who would later find happiness with two consecutive wives, but John Kelly was just finishing off a divorce caused in part by the conflicts between his marriage and "the Job." And Kelly saw the Job-with-a-capital-J as encompassing far more than just the individual cases that came his way. For Kelly the world itself was infected and needed to be cured. Every person who crossed his path was in need of being saved, and it was his job to save them.

This shouldn't suggest that he was successful. Like Sisyphus, Detective Kelly pushed the rock up the mountain, making every effort to protect his charges from the grim realities of modern life. And more often than not, like Sisyphus, he got to the top of the mountain only to see the rock tumble back downhill. Kelly's victories were small ones; meanwhile the sad, tired, absurd world dragged on despite his efforts.

Detective Kelly's single-minded obsession with saving the world made him a bit monochromatic as a character (and it must be said that David Caruso played monochrome very well). Andy Sipowicz was, and is, *colorful*. Andy was drunk, Andy was racist, Andy had a temper.... In the variety of personal traumas of Andy Sipowicz's life lay countless tales which would fit nicely into a one-hour timeslot. John Kelly had angst. He had it last week, he had it this week and he would more than likely have it next week as well.

Therein lay the other difficulty with Kelly as a continuing character: he was never going to be cured. Over time, Andy could conquer his various demons and find a semblance of happiness. He had specific ailments with specific solutions. The world of *NYPD Blue* might be as bleak in its second decade as it was in its first, but the audience could see the growth in Sipowicz and believe things were gradually getting better. Kelly lacked a specific ailment. He didn't really have demons; he just lived in Hell. And Hell wasn't going away, not in season one, not in season two, not ever.

All of this made Kelly a fascinating character and lent depth to an otherwise fairly standard cop show—naked butts notwithstanding. *NYPD Blue*'s nudity might have gotten people's attention, but it was Kelly who made it worthwhile to stick around once everyone had their clothes on. Two problems arose, however: Caruso was rumored to have a prickly demeanor with his coworkers and was apparently anxious to transfer his new status as series star to film. He left the show early in season two and was replaced by the excellent Jimmy Smits. This solved the other problem, which was more fundamental: what do you do with Det. John Kelly in seasons three, and four and five?

Smits' Bobby Simone was an easy character to invite into your weekly life. He was up against some serious audience skepticism when he moved onto the show; he was that smoothie from *L.A. Law* replacing Kelly the Hero. But Smits himself eased the transition with his stellar work as Simone: good-looking, friendly with a hint of mystery, always willing to reach out to someone in need but equally as ready to play rough when the situation required it.

Nonetheless, the transition from Kelly to Simone (and from Caruso to Smits) was not the major transition for *NYPD Blue* in that second season. The primary change was from a Kelly-centric show to a Sipowicz-centric show. With the arrival of Jimmy Smits, *NYPD Blue* became "Andy and His Friends." (Unofficially, of course; officially, Smits got top billing over Franz.) In the first post-Kelly episode, Andy freaked out over this unknown new partner, reflecting the audience's own feelings. When, by episode's end, Andy had begun to make a positive connection with Simone, the audience felt reassured: the new guy was a good guy; Andy liked him.

This established a pattern to which the show has continued to adhere. No one is fully trusted by the audience until Andy trusts them. As Andy changed partners over the years, the same thing happened: the audience wondered how the new guy would fit in, Andy Sipowicz wondered the same thing; Andy came around, and the audience did, too. (This has held for secondary characters as well; once Andy offers up one of his rare but patented "you're a good cop, Medavoy" numbers, our confidence in that character increases.)

This wouldn't have worked for Kelly. One of Andy's most consistent characteristics is that he is resistant to change. So every time he gets a partner, Andy gets grouchy, setting the stage for the "coming around." John Kelly, on the other hand, gave everyone the benefit of the doubt, at least at first—he didn't start at ground zero with new people like Andy. Kelly was also consistent (drearily so for those who weren't taken by his character): his worldview was downbeat, and he would never "come around."

Jimmy Smits was able to coexist in this new *NYPD Blue* because of his excellence at underplaying. Although the character of Simone often took a backseat to Sipowicz in terms of the show's central focus, Smits somehow managed to show intelligent caring through little more than twitches of his upper jaw. This was probably more work than it appeared; Smits must have known how good he was, how deserving of a meatier portion of the show, but he was a good company player—he let Franz win all the Emmys (not to say that Franz wasn't deserving) and contented himself with the jaw twitch and the occasional sex scene with Kim Delaney.

Eventually Smits, like so many actors on *NYPD Blue* not named Dennis, realized the program wasn't really giving him the acting opportunities that he deserved, and he left the show. (When Esai Morales left, he could have been speaking for a decade's worth of actors when he was reported to have said, "My management and I decided, if I'm going to be off the market for features and other shows, I should have a more substantial part. I'm going to be off the market, let me make some Dennis Franz money or get that kind of screen time."[1]) Smits, at least, went out with a bang: the five-episode arc where Bobby Simone died of heart problems was excruciating in an exactly appropriate way. It is hard to imagine a more honest portrayal of death and mourning in series television, with the possible exception of "The Body" from *Buffy the Vampire Slayer*. And, it must be said, the act of dying perfectly suited the style of acting Smits had perfected over the years: nearly immobile, Smits made every character in the show, and every member of the audience, believe they were seeing into his heart.

The passing of Bobby Simone also marked the passing of the notion that Andy's partners were his equals. *NYPD Blue* had centered on Andy

---

[1] http://www.philly.com/mld/philly/news/breaking_news/7696991.htm?1c

for many years by then, but Kelly and Simone were both mature adults who at least theoretically operated on Andy's level. Andy's subsequent partners were played by actors (Rick Schroder and Mark-Paul Gosselaar) who had made their names as child stars in television sitcoms. Schroder's Danny Sorenson in particular offered a chance for Andy to be a father figure and mentor, though Sorenson had too many personal problems to really benefit from Andy's training. And to be fair, Gosselaar's John Clark, Jr., is already mostly too adult to need too much of Andy's help. Nowadays, when Andy refers to his partner as "Junior" it's more a friendly nod to a good younger cop than an attempt to adopt the kid. Still, it's a sign of how Andy-centric the show has become: the older Sipowicz gets, the younger his partners become. These partners don't really operate in the same world Andy does outside the job; their cultural references are different. And since the show itself generally takes the perspective of a man from Sipowicz's generation, when, say, Junior makes a knowing reference to hip-hop music, Andy (and through him the show) raises his eyebrows as if to say, "The kids these days." Gosselaar in particular is good enough in his role to maintain audience interest, but the increasing age differential between Andy and his partners, along with the middle-aged perspective from which the show operates, makes Andy even more central while pushing those younger partners further toward the periphery.

Only one character in recent seasons has been a true equal to Andy Sipowicz. Charlotte Ross first appeared on *NYPD Blue* during the Jimmy Smits era as a battered wife. She was good, and attracted the attention of the powers that be, resulting in her return to the show as a regular, Connie McDowell, during the Sorenson years. Ross is a terrific actress (it is one of the unnoticed delights of this show, which goes on season after season, that the cast is still so uniformly good), and with Connie, it seemed like the *NYPD Blue* creators had finally learned how to write a female character that properly combined toughness and sensitivity (Jill Kirkendall was the best previous example, until they buried her toughness under ludicrous plot shenanigans). Connie was able to meet Andy head-on; she brooked no nonsense from him and she was a capable cop on the job. Scenes between Ross and Franz had real electricity; the characters respected each other and the actors seemed to be having a fine time working together. Especially given the rut that even the best series can't escape after so many years, it seemed like a perfect pairing to take *NYPD Blue* into the twenty-first century: Andy Sipowicz and Connie McDowell, partners.

Sadly, it never happened. The two worked some cases together, but ultimately the producers made room for the obvious chemistry between Franz and Ross the only way they apparently knew how: by focusing on Sipowicz and McDowell's personal rather than work relationship in a long plot arc that culminated in the couple's wedding.

In this, as in many other areas, *NYPD Blue* shows itself to be a mostly traditional cop series, better-made than most, with an excellent cast and the occasional edge-pushing seminude scene. As cable networks make inroads on audiences, however, the edge gets pushed further away from the ABC series, a phenomenon best exemplified by the FX series *The Shield*. *The Shield's* central figure, Vic Mackey, was often compared to Andy Sipowicz during the buildup to the premiere: rough cop who gets the job done, played by Michael Chiklis, a pudgy Everyman actor known for playing John Belushi in *Wired*. The comparison didn't hold up beyond the end of *The Shield's* first episode. First, Chiklis showed up all buff (his tight T-shirts and shaved head led some to note he looked like a walking, talking penis). Then Mackey killed a fellow officer in cold blood to prevent the officer from finding out that Mackey and his crew were dirty cops. While Mackey, like Andy, was an excellent cop with a desire to make the streets safe for average folks, his tendency to go beyond what the law allowed added an extra dimension to his character, in the process demonstrating just how mild Sipowicz had become over the years.

It remains to be seen whether or not a complicated character like Vic Mackey can carry a series over extended seasons. *NYPD Blue* found the solution to that problem when it replaced the tormented complexity of John Kelly with the more standard list of personal foibles that constitutes the character of Andy Sipowicz. The expert acting of Dennis Franz and the smart casting of Andy's partners and workmates have helped *NYPD Blue* maintain a solid level of excellence over the years. But none of that would have been possible if John Kelly were still around. Kelly's existential torment, finely drawn by the writers and effectively portrayed by David Caruso, put *NYPD Blue* on the map, but it also painted the series into a corner.

Fortunately, *NYPD Blue* already had the prototype for a character that could anchor a long-lived television series: a man with problems that could be solved over time rather than a problematic man doomed to forever push a rock up a mountain. Much is made of the fact that Andy Sipowicz is the only original character still with *NYPD Blue*; in fact, without Andy Sipowicz, *NYPD Blue* would exist only in reruns.

NOTE: I owe a debt of gratitude to Alan Sepinwall for his invaluable Web site devoted to the show, at http://www.stwing.upenn.edu/~sepinwal/nypd.txt.html. Of particular assistance were the episode summaries, begun by Sepinwall and later continued in fine fashion by Amanda Wilson. A tip of the cap as well to the folks at http://alt.tv.nypd-blue.

Steven Rubio aspired to John Kelly, but never even made it to Andy Sipowicz. Henry Coffield, maybe. He currently teaches courses in critical thinking at American River College, and has been a member of the blogosphere since January 2002.

Saving Society One Broken Home at a Time: Family Ties in *NYPD Blue*

NYPD Blue has a way of confounding expectations and defying its critics. The show that was berated for harsh language and boycotted for its nudity and sexuality turns out to be about something else after all. Looking back over twelve seasons, it turns out that NYPD Blue, at its core, celebrates something that its critics never would have guessed: the family.

WHEN YOUR CHILDREN ARE YOUNG and your emotions are close to the surface, you find your worries and fears mirrored everywhere. For sanity's sake, I had to stop watching *NYPD Blue* for a while in the mid-1990s, when the drama's relentless tide of victimized or murdered kids and abusive or grieving parents became too much for this mom to bear.

I can't remember exactly what brought me back to *NYPD Blue*, but I started watching the show again in the 1997–98 season. I got hooked on the three pregnancy storylines that were being played out at the same time—unusual, given that the series had never really seemed interested in presenting a strong, credible female perspective. Plot-wise, the most significant of these pregnancies was that of Det. Diane Russell, who was carrying the child of her lover, Det. Bobby Simone. How could Diane and Bobby even think about bringing a child into the world? Every day these two cops poked around in other people's family tragedies, breaking bad news to parents, spouses and children, witnessing the grotesque remains of parental love turned perverse or lethal. Diane and Bobby could have let it all paralyze them. Instead, they chose to believe that their love would be enough to ward off the internal and external miseries that cause families to splinter. They took a leap of faith. And, really, isn't that what all of us do when we decide to have children?

In the fifth season, *NYPD Blue* began asserting its theme with boldness and persistence. True, many viewers and television critics (not to mention right-wing crusaders like Rev. Donald Wildmon) couldn't get past the show's nudity and explicit language. But *NYPD Blue* is more than bare butts and dirty mouths. At its core, *NYPD Blue* is a long, blue meditation on the family as the seed of the best and worst of human intentions. It's about the childhood roots of crime and dysfunction and the way some people can break free from damaging beginnings while others go on to perpetuate abuse and violence. It's about society as a reflection of the quality of the individual family ties within it. Most of all, *NYPD Blue* is about the preciousness—and the awful cheapness—of life in urban America.

All of these themes were hauntingly illustrated in the Emmy-winning two-part episode "Lost Israel." In "Lost Israel" (which was written by, among others, series cocreator David Milch), an affluent father who had been sexually abused as a child murdered his own young son, whom he had been sexually abusing. The father tried to frame a mute, Bible-toting, homeless man for the crime. Det. Andy Sipowicz, who was still grieving over the recent murder of his own (adult) son, suspected that the father had killed the boy. But Andy's rage at the father (how could anyone kill his own child?) hampered his effectiveness in the case; he became obsessed with combing the homeless man's inscrutable Bible passages for an explanation, or a justification, for the death of both sons. Meanwhile, Diane Russell bartered her own history as a victim of incest, using her confessions to draw out the dead boy's emotionally withdrawn mother and persuade her to incriminate her husband.

As seen in real world statistics, very few of the crimes on *NYPD Blue* are random or perpetrated by strangers—it's usually the father or the mother, the husband or the wife, the brother, sister or child who end up getting collared. The detectives' empathy often turns out to be their most indispensable crime-solving (and crime-preventing) tool. In the episode "A Box of Wendy," a newly pregnant Diane Russell investigated the death of a six-year-old boy who supposedly fell down the stairs and hit his head. The truth was that he was sent hurtling down the stairs by a punch from his abusive stepfather, who became angry when the boy refused to go outside to play.

Near the end of the episode, Diane confronted the boy's mother, who was hugely pregnant and utterly indifferent to her son's death and her husband's violence. "You know, not everyone's cut out to raise kids," Diane told her firmly but sympathetically. Her suggestion that the woman put the new baby up for adoption might strike some people as judgmental, self-righteous or just plain out of line. What right does a cop (and a pregnant one, at that) have to decide whether another woman is or isn't fit to be a parent? But in the context of *NYPD Blue*, with its revolving door procession of family violence and despair, Russell's frankness was nearly heroic. At the very least, she gave the woman something to think about, a nudge toward truly ending her family's cycle of violence. And it was a better way out than the one Diane's own mother took when she shot and killed her abusive, molesting husband.

Diane Russell and Bobby Simone never became parents together—she had a miscarriage and then, in the following season, Bobby developed heart failure (Jimmy Smits was being written out of the show). His death in the harrowing episode "Hearts and Souls" was agonizing to watch, as much for his suffering as for Diane and Andy Sipowicz's anguish as they urged him to let go and be at peace. Bobby Simone's death provided *NYPD Blue* with an opportunity to solidify the idea that the 15th detective squad was indeed a family that experienced all the highs and lows of life together.

When *NYPD Blue* premiered on ABC on September 21, 1993, it bore undeniable similarities to cocreator Steven Bochco's seminal adult cop drama of the 1980s, *Hill Street Blues*. Both shows featured large ensemble casts, multiple, overlapping storylines and roving hand-held camerawork. With its unprecedented gritty depiction of violence, language and sexuality, *Hill Street Blues* (which Bochco cocreated with Michael Kozoll) opened the broadcast network territory later bulldozed by *NYPD Blue*. The two series also shared the complex view that, in a post-Vietnam and post-Watergate America where there were no longer any moral absolutes, the lines between right and wrong, justice and vengeance, law and lawlessness, were forever blurred. On both shows, you can tell the good guy not by his white hat, but by how much his conscience torments him.

Most of all, *NYPD Blue* and *Hill Street Blues* are about a "work family," a group of unrelated people sharing a workplace who bond as a surrogate family. Indeed, throughout its run, *Hill Street Blues* anchored an NBC Thursday lineup that was made up almost entirely of work family shows, including (in various TV seasons) *Taxi*, *Cheers* and *Night Court*. The *Hill Street Blues* family tree included a father figure, Sgt. Phil Esterhaus, whose death three years into the series (actor Michael Conrad succumbed to cancer) hit the precinct hard; a brilliant but temperamental "elder son" (Capt. Frank Furillo); and a brood of younger "siblings" (sensitive Lt. Henry Goldblume, eccentric Det. Mick Belker, eternal screw-up Det. J. D. LaRue). There was also a black sheep of the family, the racist, sexist Det. Norm Buntz, played by Dennis Franz; Buntz later evolved (if you can call it that) into Andy Sipowicz.

When *NYPD Blue* began, Det. John Kelly was the father figure of the 15th Precinct's detective squad. A honey-voiced, somber, stand-up guy, Kelly had a reputation for knowing just how far he could go without crossing any lines to see that justice was served. Kelly was his partner's keeper, even though Andy Sipowicz was the older and more experienced detective. Sipowicz was at rock bottom, a divorced, foul-tempered, bigoted, self-loathing alcoholic whose personal demons threatened to wreck his career. Besides doling out tough love to Sipowicz, Kelly also played mentor/big brother to new detectives Greg Medavoy and James Martinez and lover/protector to troubled plainclothes cop Janice Licalsi.

With input from creative consultant Bill Clark, a former New York City homicide detective, *NYPD Blue* realistically portrays the familial nature of police work. Kelly's father had been a decorated cop killed in the line of duty; Licalsi's father was a cop on a mobster's payroll; future 15th squad detectives Connie McDowell and John Clark, Jr., were the children of cops. Being a cop tends to run in the blood in the real world, and so it does on *NYPD Blue*. Alcoholism tends to run in families, too, and many of the cops of the 15th squad have turned to the bottle to numb the pain of dysfunctional childhoods. Sipowicz's father had been a brutal, racist drunk; Diane was on and off the wagon throughout the show's run; Det. Danny Sorenson, who had been abandoned by his parents when he was a teenager and left to raise his younger sisters, exhibited signs of incipient alcoholism as well as obsessive-compulsive disorder (he hoarded paper clips when he got emotionally, as he put it, "stirred up").

Even those members of the 15th squad who didn't drink had plenty of reason to. John Clark was burdened with an overbearing, alcoholic, meddlesome father (who eventually committed suicide). Martinez's brother died of a drug overdose, and his father had to be dissuaded from killing his son's dealer. Lt. Tony Rodriguez tried in vain to help his ex-wife overcome her drug addiction. Yet, in contrast to the perps they arrest each week for murder, domestic violence and other crimes, the men and women of *NYPD Blue* have somehow been able to rise above personal trauma and despair. They've ended up on the right side of the law—for the time being, anyway.

According to *NYPD Blue*, criminals are made, not born; which abused child will grow up to become abusive, which grieving parent will be driven to vigilantism, comes down to the choices people make. In many ways, *NYPD Blue* has always been the story of Sipowicz's trudge toward redemption, his struggle to transcend his hate, rage and guilt. As his partners have come and gone, Sipowicz has been forced into the position of reluctant father figure, defusing and counseling young hotheads like Sorenson and Clark. Over the course of the series, Sipowicz has grown into belated manhood, and his efforts to become emotionally healthy and whole are symbolized by his dogged attempts to build a family outside the squad room.

Oh, what a life of Job poor Sipowicz has led. After his spectacular series-opening flame-out, Sipowicz joined AA and cleaned himself up enough to woo and wed assistant district attorney Sylvia Costas, with whom he had a son, Theo. He reunited with his estranged son, Andy, Jr., who decided to become a cop like his father. But Andy, Jr., was killed trying to stop a street crime before he even graduated from the police academy. Sipowicz fell off the wagon, got back on again, beat prostate cancer, endured the death of Bobby Simone and lost Sylvia when she was killed in a courthouse shooting by the distraught father of a murder victim, who was aiming for the defendant. To add to his burdens, Sipowicz had to raise Theo alone, tend to the grieving Diane Russell (he became her AA sponsor) and deal with the death of yet another partner when Sorenson was killed during an undercover operation.

Beginning in the 2002–03 season, Sipowicz finally started to catch a break. He fell in love with Det. Connie McDowell, and he and Theo eventually moved in with her and her infant niece, of whom she had gained temporary custody after her sister was murdered by her abusive husband. Connie and Andy's blended family, in which the parents weren't married and weren't related by blood to each other's children, looked a lot like many American families nowadays. But their right to call themselves a family was challenged by Connie's sister's in-laws, the Colohans, who were fighting to gain custody of their granddaughter. In the final scene of the episode "Meet the Grandparents," Connie held her baby niece while Andy laid out their options to strengthen their chances of winning custody: marry, which was against police department policies, or he and Theo could leave. "No one is going to break up this family," declared Connie.

Andy and Connie prevailed in court—after the 15th squad dug up evidence that the baby's grandfather had molested his daughter when she was a child. The daughter, now an emotionally shattered alcoholic, testified against her father only after being persuaded by another of Diane's sympathetic confessions. This pivotal development in Sipowicz's story marked another of the series' challenges to traditional religious and judicial notions of "the sanctity of the family" and the idea that blood relatives were always the preferable guardians in custody battles. Andy and Connie's nontraditional family was obviously loving and harmonious; the Colohans, although legally married and outwardly upstanding, had raised a murdering son and a damaged daughter. They were rotten inside.

In the episode "And the Wenner Is...", Sipowicz and the pregnant McDowell were married in their apartment in a ceremony performed by John Irvin, the squad's gay civilian receptionist, who had earned the respect of recovering homophobe Sipowicz. (Rather than make Andy or Connie transfer out of the department to satisfy job policy against spouses working together, Lieutenant Rodriguez gave his covert approval to the secret marriage.) Irvin, who had become an Internet-ordained minister for the occasion, blessed not only the couple, but the assembled members of the 15th squad, with a sentiment that could stand as the series' epitaph: "We come from different backgrounds. And who knows if, under different circumstances, any of us would be in each other's lives," said Irvin. "But this job has brought us together as a family."

For all of the show's gloomy examples of families falling apart, the cops of *NYPD Blue* are, like most of us, driven to find mates, have babies. The show's insistence that the love, safety and comfort of a healthy family is the best way to mend broken souls and broken societies is at once simple and profound. *NYPD Blue* started out as a cop show, but it has become the most pro-family hour on television.

Joyce Millman's essays about television have appeared in the New York Times, Variety, Salon.com *and the* Boston Phoenix, *among other publications. She was a founding staff member of Salon. She was also a finalist for the Pulitzer Prize in criticism in 1989 and 1991 for columns written as television critic for the* San Francisco Examiner. *Throughout her career, Millman has championed cult favorite shows like* Twin Peaks, My So-Called Life, The X-Files, Freaks and Geeks, Buffy the Vampire Slayer *and* Angel *with varying degrees of success. Her proudest moment as both TV critic and fan came in 2003, when she was paraphrased in a line of dialogue on* Buffy. *She lives in San Mateo, California, with her husband and son.*

SHARON BOWERS

Watching Jill and Diane: *Blue* through Other Eyes

It's a well-established tradition among hard-core television fans to speculate about sexual relationships, often homosexual relationships, between their favorite characters, even if these relationships are not exactly written into the script. Slash fiction, fan fiction that describes these "imaginary" relationships, has become enormously popular in television series like Star Trek, Frasier *and* Buffy. *But* NYPD Blue, *with its upfront sexuality and continually shifting relationships, leaves little room for slash. And, if fans somehow did imagine relationships between their favorite characters on the show, it would certainly be entirely a product of their imagination. Don't you think?*

NYPD *Blue* creator Steven Bochco has always referred to his groundbreaking television show as "The Redemption of Andy Sipowicz," and indeed, the show's main narrative concerns Detective Andy Sipowicz's struggles to find peace on the job and at home, to redeem himself for his past wrongs. The stories of the other officers, the criminals, victims and witnesses that he encounters, form an echo of and chorus to Sipowicz's trials and tribulations.

But what happens when a viewer shifts her focus? When she is drawn to the show not because of Andy Sipowicz's story, but rather those other, more elliptical stories? When the characters that rivet her attention to the screen are not named Simone and Sipowicz, but rather Kirkendall and Russell?

I first started watching *NYPD Blue* near the end of the second season, drawn to the show because I had been a big fan of Bochco's first police drama, *Hill Street Blues*. Throughout *Hill Street's* run, I was fascinated not by Daniel J. Travanti's flawed but struggling Capt. Frank Furillo but rather Furillo's intelligent and temperamental lover, Joyce Davenport. Likewise, when I tuned into *NYPD Blue*, I found myself drawn not to *Blue's* main character but instead to a then-recurring guest character, Det. Diane Russell, played by Kim Delaney.

In many ways Russell, the street-smart, alcoholic undercover cop, served, especially at the beginning, as a female mirror of first-season Andy Sipowicz. She was a cop working at the edges of her ethics, troubled by a drinking problem that not only threatened her life, but also put her new partner Bobby Simone at risk. From her introduction, Russell's character stood in stark contrast to female characters in the vast majority of television cop shows, who are relegated to the sidelines (*Hill Street Blues'* Lucy Bates) or are indisputably heroic in spite of their flaws (*Cagney & Lacey's* Christine and Mary Beth). Given *NYPD Blue's* penchant for the darker side, I honestly didn't know whether or not Russell's ragged edges would be her undoing. Diane's struggle over the tension between the familiar (drinking, being alone) and the unknown (security, love with Bobby) resonated with me and kept me watching as her story continued to unfold.

Diane's "wake-up call" mirrored Sipowicz's as well. Her turning point came when Bobby asked her not to back him up on a risky bust because she had been drinking on the job. Though her bottoming out was nowhere near as drastic as Sipowicz's—he was shot and nearly killed while on a binge with a prostitute in the series' pilot—the effect was the same. Diane set out on a long road to redemption, working toward conquering her personal demons and achieving a happy, fulfilled life.

Just as with Sipowicz's character, the show hinted that Diane's alcoholism was inherited from her father and further complicated by her troubled relationship with him. In the show, Andy's experiences with his angry, drunken father are linked narratively with his racism. Diane's alcoholism, however, was marked by her gender. In the fourth season Diane recovered suppressed traumatic memories of long-term sexual abuse at the hands of her father.

This development troubled me on many levels, both as a viewer and a feminist. Leaving aside the controversial issue of "recovered memories," this complication had far-reaching reverberations for the character. First of all, it deepened the connection of Diane's character to "sexual object/object of desire" of both Bobby and the show itself. From its inception, *NYPD Blue* has been notorious for pushing the boundaries of "acceptable nudity" on a network television show. True to form, in her first appearance on the show Diane took Bobby to bed—and Kim Delaney ended up naked. This occasion in and of itself wasn't surprising or particularly troubling. Just about everyone—from first-season series lead David Caruso to Dennis Franz himself, and all the female characters in between—has done nude scenes on the show. With the revelation that Diane was a victim of long-term sexual abuse, however, Diane's difficulties in accepting Bobby's love and moving on with their relationship became directly linked to her past sexual behavior—her father's abuse, her subsequent identification of sex with affection and her (offscreen and unseen) sexual promiscuity. This development reduces the complexity of Diane's past actions to a single deliberately "female issue," simplifying and in many ways erasing what had drawn me to this show and character in the first place. By contrast, Andy's equally troubled path to love with ADA Sylvia Costas was not cast in this kind of singular light; instead there were a number of complicating issues in their relationship. Drinking and Andy's past with his father were only two of them.

A second, perhaps more troubling, implication occurs in the link between Diane-as-victim and Diane-as-cop. While the show certainly never suggested that as a child Diane should or would have had the ability to "protect" herself from her father, the series (manifested in Bobby's overprotective tendencies and her vacillating resolution to stay away from Bobby until she "gets things under control") subtly but inexorably undercut Diane's autonomy as a cop and an individual. This feeling was amplified by the sudden and jarring conclusion of the fourth season's "Jimmy Liery" story arc, in which Diane returned to her undercover roots. Instead of Diane's weeks of work paying off in an arrest, Liery drugged her, and she confessed her worst fears—that Liery raped her—to Bobby. Predictably, Bobby went after him, indirectly causing Liery's murder at the hands of his business associates. Thus, Bobby got his man—both professionally (the bad guy was off the streets) and personally (he had been jealous of Diane's undercover work getting "close" to Jimmy). In stark contrast, Diane was left literally in a crying, shivering heap in Bobby's doorway.

I kept watching, sometimes almost in spite of myself, aggravated by the dismantling of a multi-faceted character but fortunately intrigued by the introduction of a new one. The fourth season arrival of plainclothes transfer Jill Kirkendall (played by Andrea Thompson) brought Diane's issues into even sharper relief as the narrative built to the revelation of Diane's past abuse.

Unlike Russell, Kirkendall was defined by a matter-of-fact competence and a well-adjusted outlook, as well as a marked disinterest in becoming romantically paired with any of her male squad mates. Both women were identified as heterosexual: Diane through her relationship with Bobby and Jill through her references to a lousy ex-husband and her two sons. Despite this, however—and in contradiction to most of the relationships between women on the series—an immediate connection was created between the two women in their first scene. In the season four episode "Unembraceable You," Russell, getting ready for the coming night's work undercover on the Liery case, commented offhandedly that sometimes her work—the way she had to dress and act because of it—made her forget that she was a good person. Jill replied, "From everything I've heard about you, that's what you are. A good person."

This exchange indicated that Jill—who hadn't engaged on a particularly personal level with any of the members of the squad—had chosen to (in visual terms) focus her gaze on Diane rather than one of the male officers. It also established a paradigm for their relationship to come. Jill provided a stable, grounding answer to Diane's tumultuous personal life in much the same way that Bobby did. When the two women became professional partners, a narrative parallel of Bobby/Jill to Andy/Diane was created: two sets of partners, though only one set of lovers.

The word subtext refers to the phenomenon in which viewers interpret the events of a television show and its characters based on small, telling bits of business while the show itself, through explicit plotlines and dialogue, interprets those same events differently. Usually subtextual readings play off of emotional nuances between the characters or "fill in" the gaps between scenes that the show leaves empty. In other words, subtext reads "between the lines" and "in the margins." One of the most common forms of subtextual reading identifies potential romantic partnerships—both gay and straight—between two characters who do not and will not ever have that sort of partnership in the literal text of the series.

As season six began, I found myself falling into just that sort of reading in the margins of Jill and Diane's relationship. When Bobby became fatally ill, I kept seeing Jill—who had already replaced Bobby as Diane's professional partner—as the character most viable to replace him romantically as well.

Following such a reading, there was a distinct "handing over" of Diane from Bobby to Jill implied in the season six episode "Numb and Number," when Jill was Diane's constant companion at the hospital, offering moral support and a strong shoulder as Bobby's condition rapidly deteriorated. Late in the episode, Jill and Diane were allowed to go into Bobby's room briefly to see him. Absent was Andy, Bobby's partner and the show's remaining male lead. Thus Jill—standing at the foot of the bed, a powerful and vibrantly healthy contrast to Bobby's shrunken and weakened state—became the visual and narrative partner to Diane's character in every sense.

As I considered my surprising new reading of their relationship, I began to realize this "passing on" was not a sudden textual development in season six, but rather the natural outgrowth of the deepening connection between the two women. A powerful example of this occurred in season five, when Jill entered into a romantic/sexual relationship with ADA Leo Cohen on Diane's behalf, to obtain information about then-suspended Bobby's case. Throughout seasons five and six, the two women continued to work together in cases most frequently marked by their gendered nature—rape, child abuse, women in jeopardy—that created a sort of a "domestic" space that the men of the squad did not inhabit.

One of the cases that most explicitly highlighted the kind of domestic sphere given to Diane and Jill's partnership was the season six episode "Grime Scene," in which Jill's youngest son Kyle witnessed a murder. Jill was adamant that Kyle not have to testify in open court, but she was equally adamant that they continue to pursue the case. Diane told her not to worry, that she'd "find a way to make it okay." Indeed, she even offered to make Kyle "disappear from the 5's"—the official record of the detectives' investigation—to protect the young boy. True to her word, she and Sorenson tracked down a suspect and elicited a confession in order to avoid a trial that would force Kyle to testify. The episode ended with Jill and Diane together alone in the upstairs "crash room," holding Kyle as he slept and stroking his hair. It was a singularly intimate moment, one unlike any other between partners on the show, and marked their relationship as different from other same-sex professional partners like Medavoy/Jones or Sorenson/Sipowicz.

The episode that immediately followed this one, "Show and Tell," only further emphasized Diane's choice of "partner." Diane was emotionally devastated when she realized—directly as a result of helping Jill and her son—that she was beginning to let Bobby's memory go; as a result, she turned to drinking again. The episode opened with Jill arriving at Diane's loft and seeing the unopened bottle of vodka on the counter. In a parallel with the season three episode "One Big Happy Family," when in peril of losing her sobriety, once again Diane chose not to call her AA sponsor, Andy, but instead her true partner to help her through the crisis—in "One Big Happy Family" she called Bobby; here she turned to Jill. Jill poured the bottle out and told her, "We're gonna get you some help," treating her with every bit of the same tenderness and compassion that Bobby did in the season three episode.

A mutuality existed, however, in the Diane/Jill pairing that did not exist between Diane and Bobby, where Diane was fixed as "sexual object/ object of desire." In a reversal of the Diane/Bobby relationship, where Bobby was frequently unsettled and overprotective of Diane's undercover activities, in the Jill/Diane partnership, Diane was the one most likely to exhibit overprotective tendencies. The season six episode "Mister Roberts" had Jill going undercover as a prostitute. Diane, monitoring from the surveillance van, was the viewer of the (false) sexual display and the one who decided to kick the door in early when she feared for her partner's safety. They made the bust, and when Leo Cohen reacted to Jill's undercover garb with disgust, it was Diane to whom the normally unflappable Jill turned in her anger and frustration. Defiantly stripping down in front of Diane's unblinking and unjudgmental gaze, she bitterly remarked that she wasn't going to let any man speak to her that way or get in the way of her doing her job. This was one of the few moments that *NYPD Blue* explicitly positioned Kirkendall (and Thompson) as a sexual object, with a three-quarter shot of her in a skimpy black silk body stocking, leaning up against the wall. It is also, at the time of this writing, the only time the text has not included a male character as the subject of the sexual display. Jill's anger and body were, the text silently implied, for Diane's consumption alone.

Though this episode invoked the heterosexual pairing of Jill/Leo, the two had not been seen on screen as lovers since early season five, and all Leo's appearance here did was serve notice that the relationship had ended. Thus, the only partnership of any kind for either woman throughout season six was with each other.

In season seven, Jill's ongoing feeling for her shady ex-husband—in complete contradiction to everything she'd said about him in the past— was introduced. As a result, Jill's dealings with her ex placed her in an untenable professional position, and she was forced to take her two sons and go on the run. My frustration with the show rose to the fore again here, when once more the narrative explicitly reduced a female character by defining her solely in terms of her gender and sexual past. Throughout her arc on the show, Kirkendall was never once shown as willing to be mistreated by a romantic partner or compromise her sense of integrity because of her feelings. In fact, except for the three episodes in which she was shown to be romancing Leo mostly for his information about Bobby, Kirkendall hadn't been involved in a romantic relationship with a man at all, a state of affairs that marked Jill Kirkendall as an unusual character indeed. It also makes a subtextual reading of the Kirkendall/Russell relationship all the more plausible and logical.

Diane and Jill's last scene together highlighted this subtextual reading. In Jill's apartment, the two women said a tearful good-bye, but not before Diane gave Bobby's wedding ring to Jill and told her simply, "Remember." This action accomplished several subtextual points. First, it established that Diane has, in fact, let Bobby go and found a way to honor him and the memory of their love while still moving on with her own life and loving other people. Secondly, it marked Jill as the recipient of that new love. By having Diane give Jill the ring (and still wear her own in subsequent seasons, until her character's departure from the show), the text created a "marriage" between Jill and Diane using the same terms and symbols that it used in the Diane/Bobby relationship. Unfortunately the implications of this action remained ambivalent and unfulfilled as Jill left town—on the run from IAB investigators—and was never seen again.

Though Jill was gone from the text, she remained present in a spectral way, a presence manifested in Diane's inability to establish a new and lasting romantic or professional partnership, including one with Bobby's replacement in the squad. Eventually, she took a leave of absence from the force, leaving the narrative field uncontested to Dennis Franz's Andy Sipowicz once more.

As a viewer I found myself leaving the series then as well, uninterested in the female cops who replaced first Jill and then Diane. These characters replicated the earlier, pre-Kirkendall/Russell paradigms of women defined by their romantic relationships to the male characters first and their ability as cops second, a reversion most notable in the relationship between Det. Connie McDowell and Andy Sipowicz. Their romantic and professional partnership not only echoes Bobby/Diane, but more importantly for the show, it furthers and re-anchors the show's ostensible main narrative arc, "The Redemption of Andy Sipowicz," stranding viewers who have been watching *NYPD Blue* through other eyes.

Sharon Bowers is an independent scholar interested in the intersection of narrative and popular television. She has presented papers at regional and national popular culture conferences on television texts such as Queer as Folk, ER, Fastlane *and* All My Children. *The author of the previously published novel* Lucifer Rising, *she is currently working on a book-length examination of competitive discourses of sexuality across a range of televisual narratives.*

JENNIFER PARKS

"English, Doc, English": *NYPD Blue* and Medical Ethics

What's the most dangerous place in New York? On NYPD Blue, *danger lurks on the streets, in bars, in the courthouse, even in the squad room. But the most dangerous place in* NYPD Blue's *New York is certainly the hospital, where detectives are injected with near-lethal dyes, fret over family members' leukemia diagnoses or find their bodies rejecting transplant organs. This danger is compounded by the doctors in these hospitals, who don't always operate according to the highest ethical standards. Ethicist Parks explains.*

NYPD BLUE OFFERS VIEWERS insight into the personal lives of its main characters: not only does the show depict the characters as professionals, but it also addresses weaknesses, losses and traumas in their personal lives. Of particular interest are the episodes that treat medical issues; while they help develop the characters on the show and advance the plot, they also dramatize current ethical problems in health care. In particular, the show has depicted two compelling medical issues: Andy Sipowicz's experience with prostate cancer and Bobby Simone's heart condition. The show's portrayal of these medical situations highlights deep and ongoing problems in medical interactions between patients, their families and health care professionals.

The episodes that address these issues share some common themes and messages, problems such as patient autonomy (or the right to make self-regarding choices in health care), trust between patients and caregivers, physicians' responsibility in making their patients deal with health problems, the dilemmas created by medical technology and the extreme corporatization of health care, which results in treating patients as medical "cases" rather than as whole persons. *NYPD Blue* poignantly raises the question of whether medicine as it is currently practiced has the capacity to respect patients' emotional lives and to reflect their value systems.

One of the most important ethical principles in health care today is respect for patient autonomy—or, put simply, respect for the individual patient's values and choices. We can see the importance of this principle being explored in both Sipowicz's and Simone's medical situations, in which questions are raised about what the individual patients value, how they want to be treated and what is best for them.

The Importance of Patient Autonomy

The principle of patient autonomy asserts that each rational, competent person has the right to make medical decisions that affect his life: since each person knows his own values, beliefs and preferences best, we must let him make the medical decisions that will directly affect his life. In cases in which the individual is incapacitated or unable to make decisions, the principle of autonomy allows for a family member or close friend to do so on the grounds that these substitute decision-makers would be making decisions as would the patient himself if he were physically capable.

For several reasons, the principle of autonomy is now considered essential to the good practice of medicine. First, there's a long history of paternalism in medicine. Paternalism literally means "rule by the father," and in health care, it resulted in doctors making decisions for their patients without consulting them. In the past, doctors might withhold information from patients, lie to them or dictate treatment—it was, as they used to say, "doctor knows best." The current emphasis on patient autonomy helps to prevent the paternalistic practice of medicine by requiring that caregivers take into account the patient's value system and treatment preferences.

Second, respecting autonomy ensures that patients have given their free, informed consent for treatment. Health-care professionals are now so concerned about patient autonomy that patients have to sign consent forms before staff will do surgeries or exploratory medical procedures. Almost everyone has had the experience of being handed a long, fine-print form that they never actually read, but sign anyway. Whether you read the consent form or not, by signing it you agree to the risks involved with the surgery and indicate that it is your choice to proceed. Informed consent, as an aspect of patient autonomy, makes it clear that the patient has assumed any medical risk and won't hold the health-care staff responsible for any negative outcomes.

Finally, the possibility of lawsuits now lays heavily on the minds of health-care providers. Especially in the United States, where health care is run for profit, caregivers don't want to do anything to patients (or deny patients any treatment) that could result in caregivers being hauled into court. With medicine's focus on autonomy, patients ideally get what they want, and staff get protection from the possibility of endless litigation.

With this understanding of patient autonomy in hand, we can now consider how it applies to the storylines in *NYPD Blue*. The show complicated the question of patient autonomy by presenting a scenario in which the patient (in this case, Sipowicz) refused to think about or even accept his medical diagnosis. In such a situation, the patient's right to autonomy becomes complicated, and doctors may take actions that would normally be considered "beyond the call of duty."

Sipowicz's Prostate Cancer: Time to Face the Music?

As anyone who has even once watched *NYPD Blue* knows, Det. Andy Sipowicz is a difficult man to deal with in both his personal and professional lives. But viewers see a whole other aspect to Sipowicz's stubborn, difficult character when they witness his response to his diagnosis of prostate cancer. He was in such denial about his diagnosis that he refused to return to the hospital to talk to his doctor, arrange for further testing or even tell his wife about his medical situation. In short, Sipowicz was a terrible patient. He represents a certain portion of the population that has a terror of hospitals, illness, death and most of all, losing control of his life. This raises important medical issues for both caregivers and patients. For example, in such a situation, does a doctor have a moral responsibility to *make* the patient deal with his medical condition? If the patient is in deep denial about the reality of his medical situation and refuses all testing and follow-up treatment, can he then "autonomously" (that is, freely and with consent) refuse treatment? If that patient is responding irrationally based on fear, and refusing follow-up care that will likely save his life, then should his choice to avoid the situation still be respected?

Clearly Dr. Talbot did not think so. By showing up at Sipowicz's workplace, Talbot overstepped boundaries of confidentiality and patient autonomy. Confidentiality was violated because his appearance at Andy's workplace left his coworkers wondering if something was terribly wrong—thus violating Sipowicz's desire to keep his health problems private. Talbot violated Andy's autonomy by trying to force his own conception of what was good upon his patient. While the physician thought it best to face the medical situation head-on and seek further testing, Andy rejected this approach.

Dr. Talbot further overstepped boundaries by contacting Sylvia to tell her about Sipowicz's medical situation. It was through Sylvia's pressure, and her reasoning with him, that Sipowicz finally returned to the hospital to address his medical situation. So, one might argue, all's well that ends well: the doctor's intentions were good, Andy was acting irrationally, and his wife had a right to know about his prostate cancer. Dr. Talbot's course of action essentially saved Sipowicz's life.

Still, Dr. Talbot's violations are difficult to justify—both morally and legally—in our current medical climate. That in the end Sipowicz's health was protected is not the only, or even the main, ethical concern. Rather, we should ask ourselves whether Andy's doctor went overboard in trying to get him to behave rationally, and whether the doctor's "at all costs" approach violates principles that should be closely guarded (for example, confidentiality, patient autonomy and patient trust in their caregivers). Arguably, some things in health care are so important that no good results can justify violating them. For example, a patient might prefer to die with dignity over being repeatedly resuscitated by her caregivers even though CPR might save her life. Physicians and other medical professionals can't claim that saving lives is always their bottom line, since many other moral concerns come into play.

Today Dr. Talbot would be in serious legal trouble for going to Andy's workplace and contacting Andy's wife without permission. The recently passed "Health Insurance Portability and Accountability Act" (HIPAA) sets out clear guidelines for protecting patient privacy, and the measures taken by Sipowicz's physician violated these guidelines. Patients may now request that physicians, pharmacists and any other health-care professionals not use their home phone numbers to leave medical information. They may also specify other conditions under which medical information is to be conveyed. Certainly Sipowicz had the right to his privacy at work and to keep his wife from knowing about his medical condition, whether or not others may agree with that choice. And while the law is not always ethical (and what is ethically right may not always be legal!), there is an ethical basis to HIPAA's privacy standards. Arguably, then, Dr. Talbot acted in ethically and legally questionable ways by paternalistically doing what he thought was best for Andy.

The physician's behavior also had a serious impact on his trust relationship with Sipowicz. It's no surprise that Andy no longer trusted Dr. Talbot after these interventions. When Andy had an allergic reaction to the dye during his CAT scan, Talbot responded by trying to continue to force testing. The doctor-patient relationship completely broke down. Sylvia and Andy resolved the situation by having another physician— Dr. Mondzac, whom they trusted and felt comfortable with—intervene to work with them in providing Andy's care. The series on Sipowicz's prostate cancer highlights for viewers the importance of mutual trust and respect in the therapeutic relationship, and the need to treat patients as emotional beings, not just physical ones. Sipowicz's situation was a complex blend of medical, emotional and psychological problems that required the medical staff to approach him as a complex human being rather than an uncooperative, noncompliant "case."

Simone's Heart Condition: Death with Dignity

The richly detailed story of Bobby Simone's heart failure raises many important ethical questions, such as how to get caregivers to address patients as more than mere "bodies," whether medical technology should always be applied to save lives and when it is ethical to stop medical treatment.

Simone's heart failure covered a ten-day span wherein his disease was diagnosed, he received a donor heart and suffered complications following the heart transplant. His problems began when he collapsed on the job, unable to catch his breath. Initial tests indicated that his heart was malfunctioning, but the origins of his condition were unknown. His condition quickly deteriorated to the point where a heart transplant was necessary to save his life. Through the gift of a designated donation, Bobby quickly received a donor heart from another officer who was killed on the job. But a heart transplant is an extremely risky and invasive surgery, and other complications arose that put his life at risk.

A post-operative infection caused abscesses to form in various organs in Bobby's body, including his brain. As Dr. Swan, Bobby's cardiac specialist, asserted, the resulting seizures, along with the abscesses, would kill Bobby if they remained untreated. Furthermore, Bobby's heart transplant required that he be treated with immunosupressants to prevent rejection of the foreign organ, yet these drugs made him an easy target for bacteria and also rendered useless any standard antibiotic treatment for infection that a doctor would normally recommend.

To make things worse, Simone's caregivers did not agree on how (or even whether) he should be treated. The physicians' different approaches to Bobby's condition and to his treatment are just one more compelling aspect of the program. Dr. Carreras suggested to Diane that sometimes the wisest course of action is to accept the inevitable and to prevent greater suffering that might come with further medical interventions. Carreras told Diane that, in his opinion, it would be better if the brain surgery to treat the abscess was not performed; he had the wisdom to know that there are some things worse than death. By contrast Dr. Swan recommended surgery to remove the abscess and fight for more time.

Which doctor would you want? What would you choose if you were in Diane's position, making medical decisions for your loved one? These are some of the compelling questions raised by the storyline.

Trust, Care and Dying Well

During the course of his illness, Bobby's health-care team changed hands repeatedly, and viewers got a good sense of Bobby and Diane's sense of helplessness in the face of this trauma. They were assaulted by technical medical language (on a couple of occasions Bobby asked for his diagnosis "in plain English, doc" as they related his problems in complex medical lingo); they were overwhelmed by medical technology and emergency interventions; and they were put off by some of the caregivers' lack of bedside manner. As viewers we struggled with Bobby and Diane to find any humanity or personal meaning in Bobby's medical treatment. As this storyline suggests, while some medical staff see patients as more than just bodies in hospital beds, treating them with respect and concern, such individuals may be difficult to find in an acute medical crisis when the focus becomes a person's body rather than his spirit.

Bobby's medical treatment raises many of the same questions addressed by Sipowicz's prostate cancer. The importance of good communication in health care, of trust and mutual respect and in consideration of the patient's wishes, are all raised with his illness. Bobby's dying and death also raise difficult medical and cultural issues surrounding how medicine and society respond to end-of-life issues. Here an important ethical question is raised surrounding how we ought to respond to the facts of dying and death: when one is faced with a serious medical crisis, should one fight to the very end or accept death gracefully, with dignity? In a culture in which death is a forbidden subject, and in which death means medical failure, it is difficult to gracefully accept it. Yet in witnessing Simone's illness, dying and eventual death, viewers saw the possibility of a dignified death that was not dominated by physicians, acute medical interventions and medical technology. With the help of Dr. Carreras, Diane petitioned on Bobby's behalf to stop the medical interventions and prevent further suffering for him. Though Dr. Swan resisted, this choice allowed Bobby to have a relatively peaceful death, receiving last rites and visits from loved ones, and deciding when he was ready to die. Here again, the value of patient autonomy is highlighted.

Bobby's heart condition also pointed viewers to the difference between dying and dying well. While it is a fact that each and every one of us will die someday, what remains uncertain is *how* that death will take place. Will it be peaceful and meaningful, occurring in a manner and at a time that we approve of? Or will it be traumatic and ugly, dominated by a futile fight to the death? This storyline is particularly poignant because it raises these questions about our own dying and death in the face of Bobby's experiences.

Key to Bobby's dying well was his relationship with Dr. Carreras (and, by extension, his wife Diane's relationship with the doctor). Here we have an example of what a good relationship between caregiver and patient (or caregiver and patient's family) can look like. Bobby and Diane trusted Dr. Carreras, and by contrast they quickly learned to distrust and dislike Dr. Swan. But why? What was it about Dr. Carreras that made them think that, as Diane put it, he was like "an answered prayer"? Viewers themselves could appreciate the difference between the two doctors: while Dr. Swan was a skilled expert and had a very good track record in medicine, he treated Simone's *body*, but did little to address him as a person with fears, feelings and particular values. His clinical and cold approach to Bobby's heart failure offered little in the way of empathy. Dr. Carreras, on the other hand, acted professionally, but at the same time he treated Bobby (and Diane) in a caring manner. For example, when Dr. Carreras was leaving the room after checking in on Bobby, he said he appreciated the work that Bobby and Diane did as police officers because his uncle "was also a cop in Boston." In this small gesture, the doctor indicated that he saw Bobby and Diane as whole persons, with full lives that went beyond the walls of the hospital. This small recognition can make all the difference in a doctor-patient relationship and shows respect for the patient as a person, not just a medical case.

As viewers watching Bobby's health decline, we vicariously experienced his suffering and fear. This is just one aspect of the storyline that makes it so compelling. Viewers could easily relate to the fear and alienation that were part of his serious illness. Health professionals deal with illness, dying and death on a daily basis, and hospitals are not foreign or frightening places for them. For the average Joe like Bobby Simone, however, entering the world of medicine is like landing on another planet, where the language is different and one feels lost and alienated because nothing seems familiar. The show raised this question of how we are to maintain our identities, and some control over our lives, when we are placed in a situation like Bobby's. When a person is extremely physically weak, on pain medications and seriously ill, it is difficult for him to assert his preferences and values, especially when the medical imperative is to "treat first and ask questions later." Under such conditions, patients often find it difficult to say "enough!" At those times, we need sympathetic, caring and observant caregivers who advocate for us.

Technology and the Myth of Cure

The storyline of Bobby's death brings to the surface emotions, fears and doubts that are raised by the specter of dying and death. By experiencing a tale in which technology could not rescue the hero, the myth of "medical cure" is exposed. While medicine generally purports to heal and cure patients, returning them to their former functioning selves so they can go back to their normal lives, much of medical treatment does not achieve this goal. Quite often in medicine, patients are at best left in a disabled condition even though their lives may be saved; at worst, patients may not survive at all. With Simone's dying and death we come into contact with a spiritual reality about the truly fragile nature of life and our human inability to stop the process of death. More importantly, we must acknowledge the inescapable fact that death is our universal fate. (Who ever said television only offers "light fare" for viewers?)

Furthermore, Simone's situation is instructive in warning us not to over-value medical technology. As many medical ethicists have pointed out, the fact that we have technologies available to us does not mean that we have to use them; on the contrary, in certain situations it may be *unethical* to apply technology. Oftentimes the application of medical treatments and technologies are not likely to save a patient's life, and the technological intervention is likely to cause a patient a great deal of pain and suffering, or cause a protracted death. Such was the case for Bobby as his medical problems multiplied following his heart transplant surgery. Dr. Swan recommended brain surgery to remove his brain abscess in what he thought might offer Bobby a slim chance of survival. But as Dr. Carreras pointed out, putting Bobby through further technological interventions was likely to cause him more and protracted suffering— an outcome which is arguably ethically wrong. The tension and differing viewpoints between Drs. Swan and Carreras left viewers questioning whether *quality* or *quantity* of life is more important. Indeed, this question still plagues medical ethicists, who don't always agree on what constitutes a good quality of life, or on who gets to determine when suffering becomes unbearable.

The conversation between Drs. Swan and Carreras also illustrates how the myth of medical cure can affect the way medical facts are presented to patients. If physicians want to maintain a high success rate in their practice and uphold the view that they are able to "cure" patients, it is undesirable to have patients die while under their care. Nothing better supports the notion of medical cure than having patients walk out of the hospital in a condition that allows them to return to their normal lives; as a result, doctors often do not want negative patient outcomes (like death) to spoil their medical success rates. Dr. Carreras raised this moral issue when he suggested that Dr. Swan was "trying to smuggle a cardiac fatality onto the neurosurgical statistics." In short, Carreras accused Swan of wanting to have Bobby die on someone else's floor to prevent his death from registering as a transplant failure. So Dr. Swan's insistence that sending Bobby to neurosurgery "could improve his odds to live" may actually have been a masked attempt to pass off his failure to another department. If Carreras was correct in his assessment of Dr. Swan's motives, then all of the medical advice that Swan gave to Diane was tainted by a personal concern that had nothing to do with what was best for Bobby. And given that a physician's first concern should be what is best for the patient, Dr. Swan's motives for pursuing treatment for Bobby were highly unethical.

Ironically, Swan accused *Carreras* of infringing on Diane's autonomy by claiming that Carreras had Diane "parroting his judgment" and that "Diane was just repeating verbatim the advice I take it you gave her." But Swan may have been infringing on Diane's autonomous choice by falsely presenting his own concerns as centering on Bobby's medical condition, not on his success rates. This conflict of interest—having a responsibility both to the patient and to the reputation of the transplant unit—compromised the best care for Bobby. Furthermore, Swan confused Diane's trust in Carreras' judgment as her merely "parroting" Carreras' orders. Offering medical opinion is not the same as manipulating or forcing a patient (or his decision-maker) to act on that opinion; Diane was just as free to accept and echo Carreras' opinion as she was to reject it. Being a rational, autonomous individual does not always mean that one must never accept others' opinions and advice; on the contrary, the best moral thinking involves considering the opinions and viewpoints of others, then determining where you stand in relation to them.

The tension between Drs. Swan and Carreras highlights the problems created by a system of health care where "cure" is valued above all other goods. Often, as a result, patients are robbed of the opportunity to die well, as they are subjected to an endless array of interventions meant to stave off death. Furthermore, since patients also cling to the notion of cure, many patients and/or their families will refuse to admit "defeat," and will demand treatments that are not medically recommended or that may cause undue suffering. Considered in this light, Dr. Swan's desire to not have Bobby die in his transplant unit was not so surprising, since his actions reflected the emphasis on cure that is shared by most people.

Conclusion: What's in a Name?

The titles of *NYPD Blue* episodes are notoriously witty, but they sometimes also contain deeper meanings that point to particular issues. For example, the shows concerning Sipowicz's prostate cancer have titles like "Don't Kill the Messenger" and "I Don't Wanna Dye"; the shows concerning Simone's heart problems have titles like "Brother's Keeper" and (particularly telling) "Hearts and Souls." These titles point to some tensions and ethical problems in medicine and medical treatment. First, consider Sipowicz's anger and fear upon receiving the news about his prostate and his resulting fury with Dr. Talbot, the bearer of the bad news—don't kill the messenger, indeed! This episode showed the beginnings of the terrible decline in the doctor-patient relationship between Dr. Talbot and Sipowicz, which the title strongly suggests. In "I Don't Wanna Dye," it was clear that Andy suffered a conflict between not wanting to face his diagnosis (thus avoiding the necessary testing and dye injections, not wanting to "dye") and truly not wanting to die. To avoid the one kind of "die," he had to face the other "dye," which required his participation in a physcian-patient relationship that he was avoiding. These episode titles get at the complexity of Andy's emotional and mental state in connection with his health problem.

The episode titles surrounding Bobby's heart condition point to some important features that are mostly lacking in our current health-care system. Consider the concept of a "brother's keeper": one who looks out for others and ensures that their interests and values are preserved. Bobby was lucky enough to find along his journey at least one advocate, or one "brother's keeper" in Dr. Carreras (not to mention, of course, the police officer whose donor heart literally kept Bobby alive). The actions of this doctor indicated a true concern for a fellow human being, and not just the clinical responses of a medical professional. But more than anything, the "Hearts and Souls" episode has an important reminder in the title—that, in situations like Bobby Simone's, we are dealing with more than just a heart that is malfunctioning: we are dealing with a soul, too, and all the complexities that come with being spiritual, not just physical, beings. The important question this episode raises is whether the American health-care system in its current manifestation is equipped to deal with these complexities, or whether extreme corporatization has taken the "heart" out of medical care.

Jennifer Parks is a professor in the Department of Philosophy at Loyola University in Chicago. Her areas of teaching and research interest include health-care ethics, disability theory, moral philosophy and feminist theory. She has published The Complete Idiot's Guide to Understanding Ethics *and a book on home health care entitled* No Place Like Home? Feminist Ethics and Home Health Care. *Parks has had articles appear in major academic journals such as the* Hastings Center Report *and* Hypatia. *She lives in Chicago with her husband, her year-and-a-half-old son and her pug dog named Oliver.*

GEORGE C. THOMAS III & RICHARD A. LEO

Interrogating Guilty Suspects: Why Sipowicz Never Has to Admit He Is Wrong

The real action in NYPD Blue *takes place in the interrogation room, where Sipowicz and his colleagues trick, threaten and, in extremis, beat confessions out of potential felons. They are willing to tune up a recalcitrant suspect, but only, as Kelly explained early in the series, if they really believe the suspect is guilty. Is this the way it works with real-life police? And if it is, are we happy with that?*

N YPD BLUE IS POWERFUL DRAMA, teeming with moral judgments and moral ambiguities. Crime hurts innocent people, and often the most vulnerable in our society are its victims. Criminals deserve punishment. But what limitations should exist on the moral guardians we call police? What rules must they follow in investigating and solving crime? Are they justified in using threats, lies and deceptions—even physical violence—to get a guilty "perp" to confess?

A classic (some would say hackneyed) law school hypothetical imagines a police officer knowing that the only way to save an innocent life is to use coercion on the suspect who put the victim in jeopardy. Is this permissible? At first glance, one might say not only that the police officer is permitted to use physical violence but also that he is duty-bound to beat the location of the victim from the suspect. But notice that the game is rigged: given that suspects lie to police much of the time, how would the police officer ever *know* that the suspect has done what he said, or that the victim is alive and capable of being saved? Rather than a white knight riding to the rescue of an innocent victim—say, a kidnap victim buried alive in a shallow grave—it is more likely that the police officer is Don Quixote, beating a lying suspect senseless when no victim exists or the victim is already dead.

Of course, in the fictionalized world of *NYPD Blue* (and probably the world of all television dramas), the officer *is* a white knight. Though viewers did not actually see Det. Andy Sipowicz beat the Czech-born suspect senseless in "Bombs Away," they did see enough. The suspect told Sipowicz that he had tied bombs to the backs of four victims, rich capitalists who would die unless the bombs were disarmed. When Sipowicz pulled the suspect to his feet, the suspect said, "You can't beat me in this country." Sipowicz responded, "You got your green card? 'Cause here's something they didn't teach you in citizenship class." He brought his knee forcefully into the groin of the suspect, who collapsed. The scene cut here, but it was easy to imagine what followed. When another detective asked about the suspect later, Sipowicz said, "He's resting. He had a bad day."

In the television world, as in the law school hypothetical, the game is rigged. In "Bombs Away," the detectives found four innocent people lying on their faces, scared out of their wits, bombs on their backs. The bomb squad arrived, and all was right with the world, or at least this small slice of it. Sipowicz acted out of a higher morality than the pedestrian one that would have demanded fair treatment even for suspects. The suspect later said to Sipowicz: "You feel like a big hero because you beat me and saved rich people....You can beat me only because I am poor." Sipowicz responded, "You are wrong there. This is America, pal. I'd of beat you, rich or poor." Sipowicz serves a nobler ideal than respecting the physical integrity of suspects; the relevant factor was the suspect's guilt, not his class.

What made this episode especially troubling was that the suspect's odd behavior and unresponsive answers early in the interrogation raised doubts about whether he was telling the truth about anything. The suspect's sudden switch from ineptly denying guilt to claiming that he had strapped expertly-designed bombs on the backs of four "capitalist pigs" made it quite likely that the story was just a sick fantasy. One might have expected the show to develop along the lines of whether Sipowicz was justified in believing a story that was most likely a lie. But this is television. This is *NYPD Blue*. And the suspect was guilty.

If Sipowicz was correct in believing that innocent lives were going to be lost, the use of force to extract information was arguably justified. Under the utilitarian principles of the American Model Penal Code, promulgated in 1961, an actor is permitted to violate a criminal law if by doing so he avoids a greater harm than the one the law sought to prevent. If we articulate the harm caused by Sipowicz's abusive interrogation as the physical assault on a suspect (rather than undermining the integrity of the entire police enterprise), then saving four innocent lives seems more than adequate to justify the assault.

But on *NYPD Blue*, violence and threats of violence are not limited to these kinds of life-or-death situations. The show's detectives use physical violence—what in the old days was called the "third degree"—to extract confessions in many of their cases. Even when the detectives do not actually use physical coercion, they routinely threaten violence, at least implicitly. They invoke death by lethal injection as an image during the interrogation in homicide cases. They slam their hands to the table. They sometimes slap the suspect. When Baldwin Jones was transferred to the 15th Precinct from the Bias Crimes Unit in "Along Came Jones," some of his new colleagues wondered about his ability to succeed as a "real" detective. When the time came to interrogate a suspect in a cop killing, the veteran detectives turned it over to Jones, telling him they wanted to "see what kind of chops" he had. The suspect said he knew nothing about the crime and Jones slugged him so hard he fell to the floor. "What if I ask for a damn lawyer?" asked the suspect. "Ask for a syringe at the same time," said another detective. "You killed a cop. Without an explanation or remorse, you're a dead man." The suspect soon confessed. As Sipowicz and Sorenson watched through a one-way mirror, Sorenson commented, "That's a nice interview." Sipowicz added, "I'd like to see what kind of left [punch] he's got."

The United States Supreme Court in *Miranda v. Arizona*, 384 U.S. 436 (1966), relied on the 1931 Wickersham Report and a 1961 civil rights commission report to conclude that police had long used physical violence and threats of violence to induce confessions. The Wickersham Report condemned these practices, at one point quoting the Lord Chancellor of England: "It is not admissible to do a great right by doing a little wrong." But the wrong is "little" only if the suspect is guilty. Otherwise, the wrong is huge. To turn these kinds of abusive interrogation techniques on innocent suspects is a moral wrong of the highest order.

But the presumption of guilt hangs over the suspects in *NYPD Blue* like foul city air. To be sure, not every suspect interrogated on the show is guilty. Sometimes the police arrest or question an innocent suspect (Israel in "Lost Israel," for example, and the younger brother of the killer in "He's Not Guilty, He's My Brother"). But the police always *know* when the suspect is innocent and thus never use their "heavy guns" to produce a confession from a confused or disoriented innocent suspect. It is this privileged access to the truth about guilt that permits the police in *NYPD Blue* to occupy a place of moral superiority.

Unfortunately, privileged access to the truth about guilt is flatly inconsistent with the real world. Police have intuitions about guilt, and good officers may be right most of the time. But even the best officers are wrong sometimes, and it's hard to say how many police officers do not have such good intuitions about guilt. DNA testing has proven that hundreds of innocent defendants have been wrongly convicted and imprisoned. A substantial portion of these gave incriminating statements in response to aggressive interrogation.

Early in the show's run, the writers seemed to have acknowledged the epistemological problem of obtaining certain knowledge of guilt. In "Tempest in a C-Cup," Det. John Kelly articulated a code for when it was acceptable to beat the truth out of a suspect, and when it was not. The suspect in question, Luis, had confessed to five robberies of taxi drivers but refused to confess to the sixth, where the cabbie was killed. Kelly asked a young detective, Martinez, to leave him alone with the suspect. He asked Martinez to lock the door on his way out. Kelly took off his watch and set it on the table.

> KELLY: Luis, you got to understand something. The man you killed. I knew him.
> LUIS: Hey, I didn't kill nobody.
> KELLY: (pulling down the shades on all the windows) Working thirty-two years pulling scumbags like you out of burning buildings. Worked side jobs. Make it easy on his family. His son's a cop. He works right here in the 15th. Right in this building. And you took this man's life for twelve dollars. I can't let it go, Luis.
> LUIS: I told you, man, I didn't kill nobody.
> KELLY: No more talking. The talking is over. You're going to tell me the truth right now.
> LUIS: Or what.
> KELLY: (walking around the table to be close to suspect) What's the hardest you ever been hit, Luis?

LUIS: Come on, man, get out of my face.

KELLY: Because I promise you, unless you tell me the truth, I am going to give you the beating of your life right here in this room.

LUIS: You can't do that.

KELLY: I can do that. I can do anything I want in here. Okay? Nobody's going to hear it. It's my word against your word. I will beat you, Luis, until you wish you were dead. You have ten seconds to start telling me the truth.

In a state of panic, Luis babbled about self-defense, which Kelly rejected because no other weapon was found. Finally, Luis said the cabbie was trying to take away his gun and "he didn't give me no choice" but to shoot him in the face. Kelly relaxed, as if a great storm had passed. "See, Luis, I told you we'd come out of this okay, didn't I?"

Martinez later asked Kelly "what happened in there?"

KELLY: I didn't beat him.

MARTINEZ: Then why'd he give it up.

KELLY: Because he's guilty and he knew I was willing to beat it out of him to get the truth.

MARTINEZ: So if it came to it, you would've beaten him.

KELLY: Let me put it to you like this. I never raise my hand on a guy if I think he's guilty or I'm trying to find out if he's guilty, but if I'm sure he's guilty and the case is going to walk unless I raise my hand, I do what I got to do.

MARTINEZ: Even though you're breaking the law.

KELLY: Okay, you're asking me if I believe in the Constitution. Yes, I believe in the Constitution and I hang onto that as long as I can, but in the case of a murderer like this who's going to walk, I leave my gun and my jewelry outside along with the Constitution.

MARTINEZ: And if you're wrong about this guy?

KELLY: Well then God forgive me. (pause) If you want I can make up something prettier than that, James, but that's the way it is.

To make the viewer less squeamish about Kelly's threats, the writers had Luis confess in a way that showed his guilt. This time Kelly wasn't wrong, and God can save His forgiveness for other cases. This informal code, that cops can beat the truth out of guilty suspects, is reaffirmed in a later show, oddly enough by a suspect. When Sipowicz asked the suspect in "Welcome to New York" if he was ready to go on a pudding diet, the suspect realized it was a threat to knock his teeth out. But he claimed to be unafraid of Sipowicz: "You're not willing to administer a beating more severe than I'm prepared to take because you're not certain I'm guilty of the crime." And Sipowicz did not use physical violence; instead, he played on the suspect's emotions to get him to admit that he intended only to damage the victim's car but lost control and put a hammer two inches into the victim's skull.

As the last example makes plain, the *NYPD Blue* detectives don't rely exclusively on threats of violence. They use various combinations of interrogation techniques that capture some of what real detectives do. These techniques have been studied by academics and can be grouped into two categories: positive and negative incentives. Positive incentives include appealing to the suspect's conscience and persuading the suspect that the interrogator has his best interests at heart. Negative incentives include threats, but also tactics such as lying to the suspect about the evidence they have and playing one perpetrator against another. Examples of both kinds of incentives can be seen in the interrogations in "Czech Bouncer." There, the police investigated a botched robbery in which the wife of the store owner was horribly beaten, and eventually died. The "interview" with a suspect included the following questions:

> SORENSON: You like beating up old people, Del Ray?
> DEL RAY: Who's going to want to do that? . . .
> SORENSON: Where's Terry Tate at, douche bag? . . .
> DEL RAY: Terry? (laughs)
> SORENSON: Yeah, Terry, you smartass piece of crap.
> DEL RAY: Ah, we cool.
> SORENSON: Oh "we cool" is the "B" answer, Del Ray. I don't need to be cool with you. (slamming the table next to the suspect) You think I won't pull that shade down?
> DEL RAY: Ah, don't hit on me. (smiles)
> SORENSON: I start hitting on you and that cocky smile is going to wind up down around your knees.

Later, Sorenson and Sipowicz interrogated the suspected accomplice, Terry. Here their strategy changed, and Sipowicz later complimented Sorenson on how he "tuned up" the suspect: he saw Terry's need to avoid being seen as the one who beat the woman to death.

SORENSON: Terry, when I find out a case I'm working involves multiple perps, and I've got them both in custody, you know who I call on the phone?

TERRY: Who?

SORENSON: My wife. Let her know I'll be home on time for dinner. That's cause I know one of the perps is going to flip and get himself the deal with the DA. Now I got no strong feelings if it's you who wants to sit here and profile while Del Ray grabs the keys.

TERRY: I wasn't there.

SORENSON: Course if I was you, Terry, and it's Del Ray buys the walk when he's the one did the violence, that might bother me some. If it wasn't me that kicked the old woman's teeth in (choking back tears), kicked her while she was curled up in a ball on the floor (choking back tears), her and her husband pleading for mercy. I don't know if I'd want to take the fall for that.

TERRY: It didn't happen. I didn't do none of what you saying.

SORENSON: But I'm not you, Terry. Maybe you don't mind spending the next few years getting raped in jail, having your hoop brothers think it was you got over on that old couple. (tears) For thirty-five dollars. (pause) That's your decision.

TERRY: I got to think something out. Got nothing to do with looking for no deal.

Terry later confessed that Del Ray beat the woman, that Del Ray didn't plan to hurt her but became enraged when both old white people just assumed that a black man was going to harm them. Sorenson took Terry's confession back to Del Ray, who needed a different kind of "tuning up."

SORENSON: This is a big test for me, Del Ray. It's a character builder. Having Terry's confession, seeing your good veins there to take the syringe, put the poison in you, I'd like to leave it right here. But I got to give you a chance to avoid the needle.

DEL RAY: You ain't giving me nothing you don't want to give me.

SORENSON: Much as I want to cave your head in for what you did to them people, I need to remember I'm in a job where I can try to help the weaker. Doing what I would like to do to you would cost me my position. So meeting my professional requirements, Del Ray, I'm telling you that with Terry confessing, leaving him the only one on record is you signing your death warrant. I got to be straight about that.

DEL RAY: So I was there, alright? I was in the store with Terry but he did all the violence.

SORENSON: So you know what corroboration is, douche bag? … You putting yourself on the scene corroborates Terry's statement, Del Ray. I got you, you prick.

The strategy here is obvious: use one accomplice to "leverage" the other. Paint an ugly picture of the future if the suspect does not confess—the death penalty, being raped in prison, being condemned by one's peers—then offer a glimmer of hope if the suspect cooperates. It is a powerfully intoxicating mixture, and one that police sometimes use in real life.

One wonders why *Miranda* has not done more to protect suspects, guilty as well as innocent, from these kinds of pressures. *Miranda* sought to level the playing field by giving suspects control over the investigation. The Supreme Court held that no statement produced by custodial interrogation is admissible unless the police first warn the suspect of his right to remain silent and his right to a lawyer provided free of charge. The Supreme Court assumed that suspects who felt incapable of dealing with police would invoke the right to silence or to counsel. And it seems clear that the Supreme Court (the majority and all three dissents) expected lots of suspects to do just that, making interrogation a much smaller part of police investigations than it had become by the mid-1960s in America.

Miranda was scarce in the *NYPD Blue* episodes we viewed for the purpose of writing this essay. Unlike on *Law and Order*, where detectives routinely begin reading the warnings as they make the arrest, the word "Miranda" and the ritual of providing warnings were nowhere to be seen, except in one episode from the first season. In that episode, "Tempest in a C-Cup," the warnings were given with care and a written waiver taken in a methodical way. The suspect, Luis, whose interrogation we looked at earlier, contemptuously rejected the idea that he needed a lawyer before the interrogation began.

Routine police practices, of course, are not dramatic. Perhaps the writers consider *Miranda* warnings part of the police routine, and believe the viewer will assume that all suspects have been warned off-camera and have agreed to talk. If so, it is a fictional example of a real-life truth: *Miranda* has become part of the furniture in the interrogation room, a filing cabinet to be moved around as needed in order to get to the main event where the suspect and police talk to each other. The Supreme

Court intended *Miranda* to be a portentous event, an acknowledgment that the suspect has rights equal to those of the State. Numerous empirical studies have shown, however, that *Miranda* warnings have become so routine that they have little effect on a suspect's willingness to talk.

One aspect of *Miranda* does appear quite often in *NYPD Blue*—the concept of "lawyering up." If a suspect asks for counsel, *Miranda* requires that the interrogation cease. In the real world, the police almost always read the *Miranda* warnings to suspects who are being interrogated, and suspects almost never request counsel. But in *NYPD Blue*, the prospect of "lawyering up" causes concern among the detectives. In "Bombs Away," for example, Bobby Simone left a murder suspect alone in the interrogation room because he was afraid the suspect was about to "lawyer up."

In this interrogation, Simone gave the suspect greater protection than the Supreme Court requires. What caused Simone to fear invocation of counsel was the question, "Does that mean I need a lawyer?" Under the Supreme Court's rules, this would not qualify as a request for counsel because it is ambiguous. Such a statement does not even require the police to ask clarifying questions to see if the suspect intends it as a request. In *Davis v. United States*, 512 U.S. 452 (1994), the Supreme Court rejected the argument that "Maybe I should talk to a lawyer" required the police to stop interrogating or to ask clarifying questions.

But when Simone returned to the interrogation room, he asked clarifying questions such as "Made up your mind?" and concluded with "We can't talk unless you decline legal counsel." The suspect declined counsel and soon confessed to a premeditated murder. Why would a suspect who wondered whether he needed a lawyer then decline counsel so quickly? Studies show that suspects rarely invoke the right to counsel or even the right to remain silent. And that is the reality in *NYPD Blue* as well. Two examples suffice. In "Welcome to New York," a suspect named Philip showed up at the police station "lawyered up" and wanted to talk to the other suspect (his lover). Sipowicz told Philip he had to talk to the detectives first. His lawyer said no, absolutely not. Philip insisted, and the lawyer still rejected the idea. Philip turned to Sipowicz and asked, "What can I say to make this happen?" Sipowicz answered, "'You're fired' gets it going." Philip turned to his lawyer and said, "You're fired." The lawyer started to say something and Philip screamed, "You're fired!" Philip later confessed.

Another lawyer proved futile in "Lost Israel." The father of a young boy had not only repeatedly raped and finally murdered his son, but also framed Israel, a mute homeless man, for the killing. Israel, despairing of any way out, committed suicide. Sipowicz suspected the father from the beginning, and was so obvious about it that the father hired a lawyer and Sipowicz was taken off the case. Simone pretended to believe that the father was innocent so that he would seek Simone out. When he did, Simone told him (falsely) that another homeless man saw someone plant evidence where Israel slept.

The father, without counsel present, demanded to talk to this witness. Simone had no chance to set up a phony interview since the father insisted on accompanying him back to the station, so he took a gamble: when they arrived, he told Sipowicz to arrange an observation of the homeless witness's interrogation. Sipowicz got the message and took them to observe an interrogation of a homeless man the police were interviewing for another case. Sipowicz entered the interrogation room and asked the puzzled detective if she was making any progress with the police sketch artist. After a momentary frown, she, too, played along and said great progress was being made.

Simone and the father were watching through a one-way mirror. At this point, Simone played the forgiveness card: he told the father that God forgives all sin, that with confession and remorse comes forgiveness. The combination of guilt, fear of being identified by the phony witness, and Simone's carefully staged sympathy caused the father to break down and confess that he killed his son to stop the rape he felt incapable of controlling. Simone returned to the precinct room, where the father's lawyer was furious at being kept from his client. "Your client wants to give a written confession," Simone said, and the lawyer stormed out of the room, fuming: "We'll see what he wants to give."

Despite the advice of his lawyer, the father held firm. The way the trap was set, it seemed believable that he would confess. Of course, once again, there was no doubt that he was the killer.

And once again, the specter of police violence suffuses the atmosphere of the interrogation. After confessing, the father told Simone that God wanted him to end his son's pain by killing him. Then he paused and seemed to realize the import of what he had just said. He began to sob and finally moaned, "Kill me. Please, please. Shoot me in the head."

After a meaningful pause, Simone said, "I can't."

Speaking later to Sipowicz, Simone showed that the sympathy he had projected was all an act to get a confession. He stalked angrily around the room while choking with fury: "No forgiveness for what he did! He will burn in hell for this!! But first I want him to live a good long time so he will wake up crying and screaming for what he did. He asked me to shoot him. I hope that shows he knows there is no forgiveness for what he did."

Sipowicz, after a pause: "He asked you to shoot him?"

"Yeah."

"He asked the wrong guy."

So what should the viewer understand about *NYPD Blue* interrogation in relation to interrogation in real life? First, that most of the *NYPD Blue* dramatizations comport with what is known about the psychological aspects of contemporary police interrogation. The police use every psychological tactic that they think will work, including, sometimes, threats and verbal coercion, and as a result most suspects wind up saying something incriminating. These scenes score pretty high on verisimilitude. On the other hand, most of the *NYPD Blue* interrogations that we observed do not reflect what is known about contemporary interrogation when it comes to physical coercion, a regular staple of the episodes we viewed. Violence, assaults and threats occur far more frequently in *NYPD Blue* than studies of real interrogations suggest. This could be dramatic license, though perhaps the New York Police Department uses violence more frequently than most departments. The New York Police Department has, after all, been criticized for violence from the days of the Wickersham Commission Report in 1931 to the Mollen Commission Report in 1994. Moreover, the physical aspects of interrogation and threats have been basically endorsed by *NYPD Blue*'s cocreator and police consultant (David Milch and retired NYPD Det. Bill Clark) in their 1995 book, *True Blue: The Real Stories Behind* NYPD Blue.

The higher ranking officers in the show seem willing to accept the idea of doing whatever is necessary to get the confession. Sorenson gets in trouble for "tuning up a suspect" too harshly when an assistant district attorney sees the suspect's battered face in a lineup. The DA's office and the police captain come down hard on Sorenson, who is suspended. But no one in the precinct, not even the head of the precinct, Lieutenant Fancy, says anything other than that it was stupid of him. Not wrong, just stupid. The message seemed to be that his mistake was not in administering the third degree but for getting caught by someone outside the NYPD.

Is this the moral world we want our police to occupy? Do we want police to lie, trick and scheme—much less use physical violence—to get guilty suspects to confess, even assuming these strategies never persuade the innocent to "give it up"? Because it assumes a moral superiority on the part of the police, *NYPD Blue* cannot sufficiently analyze these questions. It cannot even begin to ask them.

George C. Thomas III is a professor of law and Judge Alexander P. Waugh, Sr., Distinguished Scholar at Rutgers University, Newark, where he teaches criminal law and constitutional criminal procedure. He has a law degree from the University of Iowa and a doctorate in law from Washington University in St. Louis. He is the author of books on double jeopardy, on Miranda v. Arizona *(with Richard Leo), and on the law of criminal procedure (with Joshua Dressler). He is also the author of over fifty articles and essays appearing in major law journals.*

Richard A. Leo, Ph.D., J.D., is an associate professor of criminology, law and society and psychology and social behavior at the University of California, Irvine. He has conducted extensive research and published numerous articles on police interrogation practices, Miranda *requirements, false confessions and miscarriages of justice. He is the recipient of The Ruth Shonle Cavan Young Scholar Award from the American Society of Criminology and The Saleem Shah Career Achievement Award from the American Psychological Association and the American Academy of Forensic Psychology.*

KENNETH MEEKS

Racism and Reality in *NYPD Blue*

In his seminal work Driving While Black, *Meeks addresses the issues that African Americans face every day on the streets—racial profiling and racist cops. In this essay, Meeks explores the complex character of Andy Sipowicz and considers whether cops like Sipowicz should even be on the force... or on television.*

I N FEBRUARY 1999, four New York City policemen searching for a rape suspect arrived at Amadou Diallo's door to question him. When Diallo reached inside his jacket, the police officers shot at him forty-one times, hitting him with nineteen bullets. The object Diallo was reaching for turned out to be his wallet.

A year later I was part of a weekend protest march. It was Sunday, February 26, 2000, and New Yorkers—particularly black and Hispanic New Yorkers—were protesting the previous day's court decision that acquitted the infamous Bronx Four, the four plainclothes police officers responsible for killing Amadou Diallo. The protest was relatively peaceful in my neighborhood that Saturday, though published reports counted ninety-something arrests across the city.

The acquittals frustrated us all. Members of the NYPD had gunned down another person of color, someone who was merely standing in the entryway of his apartment building. We thought a jury would have at least slapped the officers on the wrist with probation, a fine and some jail time. But nothing! The acquittals underscored the relationship between the NYPD and New Yorkers of color, and it was a very black versus white issue. The officers of New York's mostly white police force had guns, badges and the license to kill people of color with impunity.

There has been a gulf of distrust between our community and the NYPD for decades, and acquittals like this only exacerbated the problem. When the residents of a community don't trust the police—the very agency hired to serve and protect—it damages our democracy to its core. The tensions were particularly high in the 1990s during Mayor Rudolph W. Giuliani's administration. While the world might remember him for his command handling of the 2001 World Trade Center attack, many people of color can't forget that under his administration the NYPD—particularly the Street Crimes Unit—developed a reputation for engaging in racial profiling. They stopped a disproportionate number of African Americans and Hispanics for "suspicious behavior," or when searching for illegal contraband. When you live in a community where the police look upon its residents as criminals, this kind of daily abuse gives you real-life NYPD blues.

When I look at the real-life NYPD, I see little improvement since the night Amadou Diallo was killed, despite the police reforms that have taken place since. Each year over 100 people come to 1157 Diallo Place (formerly Wheeler Avenue) in Bronx, New York, to mark the anniversary of the tragic NYPD-Diallo shooting. We must never forget.

In our community, we warn our young black men against the deadly potential of even routine police encounters. This is the reason why I wrote the book *Driving While Black: What To Do If You Are A Victim of Racial Profiling* (Broadway Books, New York). Too many of our young black men were being shot by police officers for no legitimate reason. I've been a victim of racial profiling by the NYPD on several occasions, and each time it left me angry, bitter and wanting to take action.

The concept behind *Driving While Black* was to help provide our children with the resources and guidelines to live through these encounters with the police. It's so important that young people know that when they are stopped by police officers, they must put aside their egos so that they don't get killed while in police custody. They need to know especially that when they are stopped by a police officer, they must remain calm and polite, and keep their hands in sight so that an officer doesn't think they are reaching for a weapon. We've learned that while the NYPD is sworn to protect us, it can without warning become the most deadly threat we face.

The NYPD that appears on network television in *NYPD Blue* captures a lot of the frustration and social problems (e.g., race relations, community mistrust, racial profiling, etc.) that New Yorkers of color have to deal with everyday. It's a sanitized version of real life, but still compelling enough to capture my attention.

The drama of the *NYPD Blue* series comes in the redemption of Det. Andy Sipowicz. He sets the tone for each episode. A hero who is flawed in so very human ways, his demons are as real and believable as mine are to me. I respect Sipowicz because he is—like me—striving to be a better person, trying to be a good citizen in our society. It's through his dialogue that we hear the moral of a story or the morality of life. In spite of his flaws, Sipowicz is a good person with a clear mission: to solve crimes, even if he has to "beat the hell" out of a person to do it. Some people are called to be accountants; others are called to be preachers. Andy Sipowicz was called to be a detective.

One's first impression of Andy Sipowicz is of a short, balding, ordinary man on the edge of retirement. He wears short-sleeve, button-up shirts and a tie—probably a clip-on. But Detective Sipowicz breaks the mold with his condescending—almost anti-what-the-world-thinks—attitude toward colleagues and the public in general. While his fellow detectives are lean, mean, well-groomed athletic types, Sipowicz is not. He's a recovering alcoholic with a nose for mystery. Despite all of his flaws, or maybe because of them, we relate to Sipowicz.

Put him in a room full of black people and we have another story. His character is very old-school, very white and clearly working-class. He keeps a small American flag on his desk, and his attitude is anti-immigrant, anti-poor and anti-African American. In essence, he's a racist—and it bothers me that he's a member of the NYPD, even in a fictional universe. It's extremely offensive that Hollywood has made a hero out of someone who is a racist by nature. This is not the image we as black people need to see on a regular basis. It's bad enough that many people of color already believe police officers and detectives are racist; a racist NYPD is a problem many New Yorkers of color have had to deal with in real life, and under the Giuliani administration, everyone associated with the NYPD was considered a racist. We don't need to see it reinforced and materialized in our living rooms. Imagine the negative message this sends to our community: the people hired to protect us, it turns out, really don't like us.

But I will acknowledge this: Sipowicz grows. I have devoted a large part of my life to fighting racial profiling, and I have seen law enforcement officers again and again cross the line between responsible police work and actions based on personal bias, a line I firmly believe no law enforcement officer should ever cross. Sipowicz is a dedicated and honest detective—and one who has crossed that line on numerous occasions. But somehow I manage to forgive him, because he continually learns something new about himself and life, and he's always doing it for the right reasons (and because, after all, it is fiction). His character starts at one point, and because of a series of events during the course of his homicide investigation, he undergoes a transformation. By the end of the storyline (though that may be several episodes later), he has learned something new, and we learn from him.

In the early years of the show, Sipowicz was deeply prejudiced. He confessed to having lifelong problems living with "them people." ("Them people," of course, was his reference to African Americans.) He said he had to fight his whole life to keep his lunch money; that he had nothing but bad days from "them people."

When his working-class neighborhood began integrating with African Americans, Sipowicz described it as blacks pissing away his neighborhood. He blamed the entire Negro race for what happened to his father, who supposedly lost an eye because a drunken African American didn't want his gas meter read. A black man, Sipowicz had always believed, hit his father in the eye with a hammer. But Sipowicz later realized that his father's story was a lie. His father, fired from the gas company, got drunk and tried to read the gas meter at a black man's house in the middle of the night; the man injured him while defending his property. This realization was the beginning of Sipowicz's transformation: the very basis of his animosity toward African Americans was rooted in a lie.

A little African American girl named Hannah helped Sipowicz move even futher toward changing his racially prejudiced views. Hannah was the daughter of a black community activist named Kwasi. Sipowicz and Kwasi had previously had a racial altercation involving the "N-word." After a series of complicated events that led to Kwasi's murder, Sipowicz tried to make a peace offering to the little girl, who had just learned her father was dead. It was a fragile moment in Sipowicz's character development. I believe he honestly tried to look beyond the race of this little girl and see her humanity, not her skin color.

But the tables turned. The girl's mother rejected his offering because of his fight with Kwasi. Though Sipowicz tried to make amends for his prejudices, racial prejudice still kept Hannah's mother from accepting Sipowicz's attempt at making things right. This scene demonstrated just how stupid racial prejudices are, and how they interfere with human compassion.

Racial stereotyping is a natural response to dealing with unfamiliar differences. We may not be able to escape it, but ultimately, we have to try. If Sipowicz can try, so can we. Despite my reservations regarding Sipowicz as a role model, it's good to see someone on television struggle, however imperfectly, to escape the racism he inherited from his parents.

In more recent seasons we have frequently seen Sipowicz looking beyond race. In one episode, a Russian woman named Virginia was having an affair with a black man named Vernon McGee, who was in love with her. In the beginning of the episode, she came across as a victim; her husband had just been killed. Virginia's husband had caught her and McGee together and, as Virginia explained during an interview with detectives, had became so irate that a struggle broke out between the three of them. The husband was shot and killed. Virginia told the police that McGee, the black man with a violent history, killed her husband.

McGee, in another interview room at the same time, told a different story. Virginia killed her husband in self-defense, he believed; he only helped her eliminate the evidence. It became clear that McGee was supposed to be the fall guy in the death of Virginia's husband. He was set up. Virginia's affair with McGee was a farce, designed to play directly into society's willingness to blame black men, especially black men with a criminal past. (Remember, Susan Smith tried to set up every black male in her community when she told the world that a black man carjacked her, kidnapped her children and later drove the car into a lake with her kids still inside.) Vernon McGee really loved Virginia; race meant nothing to him. Yet his race was used against him.

I give Sipowicz credit for looking past the racial stereotype (including the fact that McGee had a violent, criminal past). As Virginia was interrogated, she eventually revealed her true prejudices and referred to McGee as a "monkey" when he refused to take the fall for her.

In this episode the producers and writers of *NYPD Blue* surprised us. The African American DA urged that McGee be arrested because in a "he said, she said" situation he would be much easier to convict. But Sipowicz decided to arrest the white Russian woman. It was a bold decision, something I hadn't expected in prime-time programming. He followed his instincts and the opinion of his colleague, a black detective who witnessed just how prejudiced the Russian woman really was. And when Virginia was arrested, she referred to the black detective as an animal—"that baboon." She asked, "This is America, where animals stick up for animals?" And as she passed Detective Sipowicz, she turned toward him and said, "You too." This scene marks a new era in Sipowicz's character development with regard to race and prejudice. Virginia's association of Sipowicz with the black detective and her former lover reflected a new step in Sipowicz's evolution; Sipowicz had learned to see people as people. The issue was no longer black versus white, but good citizens versus bad citizens. Race no longer mattered. Ironically, Virginia became the animal as she was lead into a cage for killing her husband and trying to blame a black man.

About the same time as the Amadou Diallo shooting, another police shooting, this time in Providence, Rhode Island, rocked through the news and virtually tore a black police family apart. A white uniformed officer killed a black, off-duty officer whose father was, at the time, the Providence police chief. Around one in the morning, the off-duty officer came on the scene to assist in a violent arrest and was mistaken for a criminal with a gun. The off-duty officer was killed before he had a chance to identify himself. The incident was devastating because the off-duty officer's father, as police chief, couldn't express his outrage toward the very police department responsible. Yet his wife couldn't accept that her husband remained quiet on the issue. Their son had been killed by one of his own classmates from the Police Academy.

NYPD Blue tackled a similar story when a white officer, Szymanski, shot a black plainclothesman five times because he thought the black undercover officer was a criminal. Five bullets are considered excessive by today's standards, but there was enough ambiguity surrounding the circumstances to create room for doubt about the degree of Szymanski's negligence. Then the writers took it a step further. They gave Szymanski a negative history with blacks, including an episode a few years earlier in which he had stopped Lieutenant Fancy in what was a clear instance of racial profiling. In fact, Fancy had Szymanski transferred to his precinct, partly as punishment, but also partly so that he could learn to deal with people of color.

When faced with having accidentally killed one of his fellow officers, Szymanski confessed that five years earlier in Brooklyn, New York, three black guys had jumped him and his wife and tried to cut off his trigger finger with a penknife when they discovered he was a police officer.

Szymanski asked, "Was I looking back at those three black kids? Maybe I was. And maybe that's what got that black plainclothesman shot five times." It was an ominous confession, especially considering that in that same scene he added, "Sure, if the plainclothes cop had been white, I probably would have given him a better chance of being on the job." This is frighteningly true to life.

Situating the incident in this manner gave the shooting a whole different spin that the world at large needed to be made aware of. We've all heard about the problem of racial profiling, but *NYPD Blue* brought the issue into the homes of millions of white Americans who will never experience it. When racial prejudices are a part of someone's history, they eventually come out…and when the person has a gun and a badge, it always comes out in violence, and often death. In real life, just as in *NYPD Blue*, there are always early warning signs. Every officer who commits a serious racial profiling offense has a number of more minor incidents in his past. In real life with real officers, with real lives on the line, we have to look for these early warning signs.

When I watch *NYPD Blue*, I see a true-to-life New York. The fast-paced movement of the camera from one on-location shot to another gives the world of *NYPD Blue* a sense of reality and constant action. It's as though I were standing in the scene witnessing the action firsthand. I don't suggest that *NYPD Blue* is quasi-reality television, but I do believe it has a very realistic edge.

Daily life in *NYPD Blue* centers around the 15th Precinct in downtown Manhattan, a stone's throw from Ground Zero and around the corner from a nightclub I used to visit back in the day. In real life, I probably passed the station house a hundred times, and if I were a character on the show, I would have passed Detective Sipowicz on the street a dozen times. If I had heard in 1993 that a police show centered around that station house would air, I would have snubbed my nose at it. I would have said it could never capture the real issue of crime as it takes place in New York City. But I would have been dead wrong. *NYPD Blue*'s ensemble of diverse actors and characters is everything hip, current and off the hook. They deal with criminal issues that affect our turn-of-the-century society, blending racy dialogue and gripping action with shrewd social commentary.

What makes *NYPD Blue* so compelling is what we learn from it about the real world. We learn about how the criminal justice system works inside a police station: the relationship between prosecutors and police officers, and the deals being made and negotiated outside the courtroom. We even see how police officers take shortcuts, and how they allow little white lies and omissions to whitewash the truth in subtle ways. We also learn how racial issues are grappled with everywhere within the criminal justice system. The way officers and detectives are portrayed on the show is exactly how I see them operate, especially toward African Americans and other minorities, in real life. They are condescending, rude and downright hostile to people of color in most cases. They treat us like criminals, like delinquents who add no value to civilization, and I applaud the show for throwing that back in society's face and saying: "Look at what racism looks like. Racism causes a lot of damage."

So what does *NYPD Blue* tell us about racism and reality?

In real life, blacks have always been fearful of walking into a police station. NBC documented this in a *Dateline* special where the network wired a young black man with a hidden camera and a microphone and sent him into a variety of police stations on Long Island, New York, to get a civil complaint form, something that should be handed out to the public with no questions asked. However, the man was questioned, and threatened with being held for not answering the questions asked by an officer stationed at the front desk. This is why real-life blacks are taught at an early age to stay away from the police. The police are not our friends. In one episode of *NYPD Blue*, a young black girl walked into the station with information about a murder. Instead of listening to what she had to tell them, two female detectives treated her like a criminal. Twice she was grabbed, and when she tried to leave of her own free will, they stopped her from doing so. I find this police action hostile and disrespectful. And it happens in real life all the time.

I remember asking myself once while watching *NYPD Blue*: what would Detective Sipowicz have done had he come across Amadou Diallo that fateful, fatal night in 1999? Would he have made the same mistake as the Bronx Four and added to the hail of bullets? In the early episodes of the show, I feel confident that Sipowicz's character would have participated in the shooting. But near the end of its twelve-year broadcast, I think he would not have. He might have even prevented Mr. Diallo from being shot. The integrity of Sipowicz's character could have been the difference between Mr. Diallo living or dying that night.

Now that the show is approaching its final season, we can look back on how much Detective Sipowicz has changed over the years, particularly in regards to racial issues. And I'm encouraged by his change. If he can redeem himself, I am hopeful that racist people watching the show can redeem themselves, too. Some people will never change. But some will. And that should give us all hope.

> *Kenneth Meeks is the managing editor of* Black Enterprise *magazine and the author of* Driving While Black: What To Do If You Are A Victim Of Racial Profiling. *He lives with his family in New York City.*

MAURICE BROADDUS

Fancy Footwork

Like it or hate it, most will agree that NYPD Blue *is one of the most daring shows on television in portraying the complex issues of racial conflict on the streets and in the squad room. Much of the attention is focused on Andy Sipowicz, whose racial issues flare up continually in the first six or seven seasons. But perhaps even more interesting and complex, if less controversial, is the portrayal of Lt. Arthur Fancy. Fancy has managed to rise to lieutenant in the racially charged environment of the NYPD. He can at times respond violently when confronting racism, yet manages to find respect for reforming racist Andy Sipowicz. Broaddus explains.*

"No one's always a liar and no one's always corrupt. Everything is a situation. You keep people out of situations and you keep them out of trouble."
        —Sergeant Martens, IAB ("Cold Heaters")

L IKE IT OR NOT, the society we live in is marked by racism. Nowhere is this more apparent than in our criminal justice system. I imagine that television executives don't want to raise this volatile topic for fear of offending their audience, and thus racism is rarely addressed on television. When it is, it's presented in a saccharine, after-school-special fashion: *"Joanie and Chachi learn that racism is a bad thing."*

But what if a show didn't care about offending you? Or even better, wanted to get right in your face and confront you with racism in all of its ugly glory for you to confront and deal with? Such is the case with *NYPD Blue*, a show that deals with issues of racism head-on.

Sipowicz is often discussed as one of the few racists on television, and possibly the only racist hero. This is a tricky issue, especially for African Americans. Many people disliked *All in the Family* because they thought that making a racist sympathetic, even to make light of him, could potentially make people comfortable with their racism.

But I'm okay with Sipowicz because no one on *NYPD Blue* is comfortable with his racism: not his wife, his partners or his boss. No one cuts Sipowicz any slack for his behavior, language or attitude.

Initially Sipowicz believed that as long as he did his job without his attitude affecting his work, his thoughts were his own. But he was often held accountable for these thoughts. The most obvious example of this can be found in the relationship between Sipowicz and Lieutenant Fancy.

Fancy plays a critical role in *NYPD Blue*'s racial dynamic. Balanced, fair and thoughtful, he serves, as much as anyone does, as the conscience of the show on racial matters. Fancy's personal and vocational respect for Sipowicz allows us to suspend our judgment. If Fancy can give Sipowicz a chance to redeem himself, so can we. We give Sipowicz the same slow, begrudging respect that Fancy does. And sometimes we just want to kick his ass, like Fancy does.

However, Fancy is no saint. He has his own share of racial issues.

In Chris Rock's Emmy award-winning comedy special he posed this question: "Who's more racist, black people or white people?" The answer: "Black people, because while each group can hate the other, black people hate 'niggas' too." In his follow-up special he asked who was the most racist kind of person, and answered, "Old black men, because they came up when times were really bad and are still bitter about it." Like "old black men," Fancy earned his rank by rising through the racially-charged New York Police Department.

What seldom gets much notice is that Fancy took hits on racial issues from all sides. It's hard enough being a black man in the workplace without serving as target practice from "your own." Fancy continually withstood insults from African Americans who felt he was more "blue" than black. He took crap from Brother Kwasi because of his decision to not fire Sipowicz. His fellow black lieutenant, Joe Abner from the Bias Unit, dealt him a sleight because he still had Sipowicz working for him. When Lewis Futrel, a black man suspected in a case of a particularly brutal homicide, didn't like the tone of the interrogation or the way that Sipowicz worked the case, he went after Fancy (who had sided with Sipowicz), saying, "They let you work in the big house now, boy?"

Sellout. House nigga. Uncle Tom. These epithets sting like the word "nigger" in a lot of ways. But black suspects, black civilians and black colleagues casually tossed these words in Fancy's direction when he made a decision they didn't like. These were the insinuations Fancy dealt with on a regular basis. The easy thing would have been to choose between being a "blue-first" cop (playing into the black community's perception of him) or a "black-first" cop (playing into Sipowicz's and other white cops' perception of him). Instead Fancy made decisions on a case by case basis according to his conscience.

Though he managed to rise through the NYPD to the rank of lieutenant, getting there meant that he had to eat a lot crap of to achieve a position where he could make a difference. He did so with his sense of fairness and self-esteem intact.

In "Innuendo" Fancy managed to take shots from his black *and* white colleagues when his brother found himself in a jam with the sergeant at his precinct. His brother got baited (the sergeant treated him "like a field hand," ordering him to change a tire when there were four other able-bodied white cops present) and fell for it in a big way (he called the sergeant a "red-faced donkey son of a bitch"). The sergeant then had enough ammunition to discipline him or end his career on the basis of those comments. But Fancy's brother had "too much integrity to let these fools talk to [him] any kind of way" and didn't want his brother "bowing and shuffling" on his behalf.

It is a Sisyphean task to be a black man in a mostly white environment and react to every single instance of racial insensitivity. It's exhausting, and one's energies get wasted in many meaningless battles. Fancy's brother asked him to speak with the sergeant to mediate the dispute; he later asked Fancy if the sergeant made him "lick the shine off his shoes." Fancy answered calmly—and with the dignity that comes with knowing one's own self-worth—"He made me lick a little." Fancy then admonished his brother to "get enough self-respect so that when some fool talks to you like a nigger you don't go half nuts and jam yourself up needing to prove he isn't right....When I hear an ass out in the field braying, I don't feel any deep need to start braying back."

Fancy's sense of self-esteem and his love for his brother allowed him to "lick a little" without losing his fundamental self-respect. However, even Fancy could be pushed over the line.

In season five's "Weaver of Hate," a white teenager was tossed off a roof by a couple of black youths. They brought in the father of the victim to be informed and questioned. Already agitated at being in a police station and wondering what new trouble his son had gotten into, he launched into a tirade of escalating epithets.

"...the element these kids are exposed to today..."

Once informed of his son's death, he tossed out a monkey reference before launching into

"...are you trying to tell me that I didn't move far enough away?"

"...and those black sons of bitches took his life..."

By the time he was punching walls and screaming about black bastards, Fancy stormed in, which only caused the man to fire off, "Are you one of those niggers jumping up and down after [O.J.] Simpson went free?"

Other officers had to restrain Fancy, warning him that they might need the father for further questioning. Still Fancy yelled out, "We don't need nothing that bad."

Fancy was not done. After learning that the DOA had been tossing around the word "nigger" right before his death, he called the father back to the station. After sharing the most recent development in the case, the father offered his version of an apology: "I've had Negro people with me since I started my business."

Fancy stayed in the interview room over the victim's objections and, in full imposing presence, leaned in and said, "...your son had to throw 'nigger' in those drug dealers' faces. And that's why he got thrown off the roof....Maybe he was thinking that on his way down: 'Wish my dad hadn't gotten me so used to "nigger" being in my mind, saying it so much, 'cause now it's gotten me thrown off a roof. It's gotten me murdered.'"

There must have been some satisfaction for Fancy in putting that racist piece of garbage in his place. But this was a father in a time of acute grief. Fancy's bullying was ugly and out of character. He defended his actions, saying that he was "past being insulted in his house."

Keep in mind, however, that Fancy also felt the pressure of other eyes; there were black people around to witness the interrogation, and he risked being judged by those who were under his command. When Sipowicz chose to confront him, Fancy refused to defend his actions and said, "When is it going to dawn on you what a joke it is, you lecturing me on my racial insensitivities?"

Fancy was human; that was his ultimate appeal. He was generally fair in the face of considerable provocation. Despite his tendency to occasionally lose his cool, the people who worked with him stood to learn a lot.

The producers' choice to pair Fancy, who had spent so much of his career overcoming racism, with Sipowicz, who was struggling to overcome his own racism, shows their sheer provocative genius. Their relationship evolved over time, but it began with their having two things in common: mutual respect and a love for the job.

When the series began, Fancy was faced with the dilemma of taking a washed-up dinosaur of a white racist cop and either putting him out to pasture or giving him the opportunity to turn things around. Surprisingly, he decided to give Sipowicz another chance.

It was no act of strict altruism that made Fancy keep Sipowicz. He knew Sipowicz was a strong, at his best phenomenal, detective. Fancy once said that of all the cops he'd ever worked with, he understood Sipowicz the best. He grew up on the job with people like Sipowicz and he felt that he could manage him. He also knew that if he got rid of Sipowicz, his white bosses would only send him another dinosaur—possibly one who couldn't do the job as well.

The question Fancy wrestled with was this: was Sipowicz capable of personal growth? At the end of season one's "Oscar Meyer Weiner," Fancy took Sipowicz to dinner at Sherman's Bar-BQ. Sipowicz, the only white person in the place, was suffering from Fancy's delight at his discomfort. Sipowicz told him that he was "entitled to my feelings and my opinion so long as I do my job the right way." However, he was operating under the delusion that blue was the only color that they needed to see.

Fancy responded by asking why the atmosphere of the restaurant made Sipowicz uncomfortable: "You're being served, aren't you, Sipowicz? They cooked those ribs for you. Maybe they wanted to spit in the plate, but they didn't. They served your white ass just like they would anyone else who came in here. Even though some of them hate your guts. So why would you feel uncomfortable, Sipowicz? You got your meal. What difference does it make what they're thinking? That they don't like you, that's just an opinion. Why should that bother you? They're still doing their jobs." Then, after a pause, he added "Now what if they had badges and guns?"

This powerful scene served as both warning and lesson about the potential pitfalls of the reality of racial politics. It also underscored something else: the measure of respect that Fancy had for Sipowicz. Obviously Fancy saw some potential, something worth reclaiming in him if he was going to take the extra time to talk with him, after hours, when it would be easier to get rid of him.

Det. Andy Sipowicz and Lt. Arthur Fancy occupied a unique place in each other's lives. For Sipowicz, Fancy was his black boss who let him keep his badge when any other would have let his boozing end his career. Sipowicz owed Fancy, and, initially, he didn't like it. But Fancy did his job well. Sipowicz himself was too fair to ignore this, so his attitude of prejudice was turned on its ear.

Even so, issues remained. Sipowicz had a low tolerance for "affirmative action policing" and even less for the "brother-brother crap" that he often accused Fancy of playing. For Fancy, Sipowicz represented all of the bigoted white cops who abused their power to oppress and terrorize his community. He represented all of the bigoted white cops who looked around in fear, seeing their power fading with the influx of different races and women invading their private club. He represented all of the bigoted white cops who had harassed and belittled him on the way up.

No one ever suggested that Fancy and Sipowicz provide a model of the ideal work relationship, but theirs was a relationship forged by mutual, if often begrudging, respect and admiration. In a world that insisted they profess that the only color is blue, the two of them had to navigate the minefield of race relations and office politics, each adhering to a code they both acknowledged.

Maurice Broaddus holds a bachelors of science degree in biology (with an undeclared major in English) from Purdue University and works as an environmental toxicologist. He has been involved in ministry work for well over a decade and is in the process of becoming a pastor and planting a church. His horror fiction has been published in numerous magazines and web sites. His television reviews can be read at the Hollywood Jesus Web site (www.HollywoodJesus.com). He is married to the lovely Sally Jo and enjoys life with two sons, Reese and Malcolm. Learn more at www.MauriceBroaddus.com.

JEFFREY SCHALER

Just One Sip for Sipowicz to Slip

Like the New York background, Sipowicz's alcoholism is a central, if not explicitly mentioned, aspect of NYPD Blue. *Sipowicz is an alcoholic, and we all know what that means. Or do we?*

"Yee doe here but sippe of this cuppe, but then ye shall drinke up the dreggs of it for ever."
— JOHN PRESTON (Breastplate of Faith and Love)

A NDY SIPOWICZ, our lion-hearted, lily-livered, existential hero, is an "alcoholic." Sipowicz is drunk in the very first episode of the series and wrestles with his alcoholism throughout the entire run of the show. Sipowicz's alcoholism has wrecked his marriage, destroyed most of his relationships and by the end of the first episode is on the verge of ruining his career.

Many people struggle with alcohol problems; these problems manifest themselves in many ways and are solved—or not—in an equally wide variety of ways. As an expert in the field of addiction and drug policy, I've studied the various techniques problem drinkers use to address their drinking—and the effectiveness of these techniques. I'll get to this later, but first I want to discuss the most widely known approach to addressing alcohol problems: Alcoholics Anonymous (AA).

AA has been so successful in popularizing its approach to heavy drinking that many people don't even realize that its approach is only one of many. AA has a very specific set of beliefs regarding what alcoholism is and how to solve it, and these beliefs are fully adopted by Sipowicz (as well as the *NYPD Blue* writers).

To understand Sipowicz one must understand his beliefs about alcoholism, which means understanding AA, and AA's views on alcohol and alcoholism.

There's many a slip 'twixt the cup and the lip

According to AA, some people are marked with a genetic predisposition to drink. Most people can moderate or control their drinking, but people marked with this genetic predisposition process alcohol differently. AA proponents speculate that about ten percent of drinkers have this genetic predisposition toward alcoholism. AA considers this predisposition a disease, a physical disease that is also symptomatic of a spiritual problem. Whether you view it as a literal or metaphorical disease doesn't really matter as far as AA is concerned. It is, essentially, a spiritual disease that lies dormant, only to emerge when alcohol is introduced into the alcoholic's body.

This is why many researchers devote considerable time and money searching for the ever-elusive "alcoholic gene." They believe that if they can identify this gene, then parents with this gene can counsel their children not to drink, as they would then be at great risk for becoming alcoholics.

If you were a fly on the wall at Sipowicz's AA meetings, you'd likely hear this story being told. Sipowicz is taught to believe that he was born with a disease that stayed dormant in his body until he began to drink alcohol. When Sipowicz started to drink it probably caused few problems, but as his drinking became increasingly regular it began to snowball into a central activity in his life. Perhaps friends asked him if he had a problem. He said he didn't have a problem, that he could control his drinking.

According to AA beliefs, this conviction that he could control his drinking marked the beginning of believing he was "God." AA doctrine says this because from its point of view, no amount of willpower can be mobilized on Sipowicz's part to control his drinking in the face of his disease. Alcoholism means "loss of control." It means that he cannot, despite any intention or sincere attempt to the contrary, control his drinking. He cannot have just one or two drinks. One drink equals one drunk.

The belief that he can control his drinking is part of what some psychoanalysts refer to as "ego inflation." That's the psychoanalytic version of the AA belief that Sipowicz thinks he's God. This facilitates Sipowicz's attempt after attempt to control his drinking. The more he tries to control his drinking, the more out of control he becomes. This becomes a terrible descent into drunkenness. Physical illness may emerge as a result of drinking—like cirrhosis of the liver or heart disease—as well as marital problems, problems at work, problems with the law, etc. As Sipowicz spiraled downward, he reached a point called "hitting bottom," a nadir of misery. At this point a religious conversion experience is most likely to occur. If it doesn't, he hasn't hit rock bottom yet. Hitting bottom is what psychoanalysts refer to as "ego deflation." (Sessions, 1957; Stewart, 1954; Greil & Rudy, 1983).

The religious conversion experience Sipowicz went through in order to come to AA involved several realizations. He said something like the following to himself and others: "I have to quit playing God. I admit I am powerless over alcohol—my life has become unmanageable. I've come to believe that a Power greater than myself can restore me to sanity. I made a decision to turn my will and my life over to the care of God *as I understand Him.*" The terms "God" and "Higher Power" are interchangeable. This process is what we don't see in *NYPD Blue*; it is what happens backstage for Sipowicz. It is the only way he could be as involved with AA as he was.

Sipowicz's joining AA was a conversion experience, of sorts. It marked a total change in identity for him. He no longer thought of himself as capable of controlling his drinking. He "admitted" that he was powerless to his disease. He admitted that he had turned his life over to God or a "Higher Power." His identity was now that of an "alcoholic." And he admitted that he must never drink again.

When the series opened, it was clear that Sipowicz had been drinking for quite some time, and he wasn't exactly a pleasant drunk. His drinking was almost certainly responsible for destroying his first marriage and clearly created a string of burnt bridges throughout the police department. Sober, Sipowicz was not indifferent to the damage he'd done. He bore an enormous amount of guilt, not only for his actions but also for the continual series of tragedies that confronted him. He was forced to face the death of his son, his wife and two partners. Sipowicz believed in a punitive God, and at some level believed these tragedies were punishment for his crimes. So when AA told him that he had a spiritual problem, he had no trouble believing it.

What also happened for him though was a special bonding with other alcoholics who had come to similar realizations. He entered into the community of AA. An integral part of membership in this community is acknowledging "the wound"—it is the wound and its acknowledgment that holds the community together. One aspect of this new sense of community and simultaneous change in identity is the formation of a relationship with a "sponsor." Another is the gradual eschewing of relationships with people who are not wounded. A third and most important task becomes one of overcoming the "pride problem."

The "onstage" Sipowicz, what we see in the show, is a man struggling to overcome his pride problem. This is the true nature of his climb to heaven, according to AA philosophy. Yes, Sipowicz must abstain from alcohol. However, that is not enough. It is not enough for him to simply abstain from alcohol ("white knuckling" it)—Sipowicz has to work to become "sober." Sobriety, in this sense, means that he has worked—or climbed—the "Twelve Steps" of AA and is living in the "Twelve Traditions," all of which constitute a deep involvement with social ritual and tenets to guide one's daily life. AA occupies a place in his life similar to the place major religions occupy in their adherents' lives. His sponsor helps him do this. His AA sponsor keeps him on the wagon. Whenever Sipowicz feels tempted by the devil—alcohol—he must get hold of his sponsor. Whenever he feels inclined to grab a drink, he must grab an alcoholic. His sponsor, at least in theory, is an "old timer," someone who has been in AA for a long time and someone who has overcome the pride problem.

In some ways, what works in AA is the sense of community, affiliation, intimacy and acceptance its members find and provide. The spiritual characteristics Sipowicz found comfort in through AA were a release from his guilt, humility toward others, gratitude for love and acceptance and a begrudging tolerance toward those he simply could not stand. These four characteristics of spirituality in AA run through Sipowicz's character.

The "backstage" Sipowicz is immersed in AA, or so we are led to believe. AA is a free, self-help spiritual fellowship of self-proclaimed drunks who gather together voluntarily to ask their Lord's blessing and to help one another stop drinking. We see two indications in the series that Sipowicz is an alcoholic in the AA sense of the word. One, he placed a high value on abstaining from alcohol in its entirety. One sip of alcohol when he met Sylvia's family was the catalyst for a devastating bender ("One drink, one drunk."). Two, he was willing, as a man who inherently resisted and resented all authority, to place himself under the authority of an AA sponsor. His AA sponsor hounded Sipowicz to make sure he didn't slip again.

"Who bent over their shoulders, to sip, before the wine had all run out."
—CHARLES DICKENS (*A Tale of Two Cities*)

In an episode entitled "Trials and Tribulations" we saw the strange side of Sipowicz's relationship with his sponsor. Dan had eighteen years of sobriety under his belt, which qualified him as an "old timer." "Who's the boss?" Dan asked. The question is multifaceted. What he meant was that the Higher Power is the boss, and Sipowicz must remember not to trust himself; he must trust the Higher Power and the Higher Power's intermediary, which—surprise, surprise—turns out to be Dan himself. Get a "GRIP," Dan said. GRIP stands for "growth," "resolution," "intention" and "purpose." These witty sayings are prevalent throughout AA and in many ways are quite useful to the alcoholic trying to stay abstinent if not sober.

But what began to leak out was a sense of Dan's own obsessions with power and control. This is a common problem among AA sponsors: they slip back into thinking they're God in relation to the person they sponsor; they become obsessed with control. Sipowicz began to sense this, and Dan's problems began to undermine Sipowicz's faith and confidence in the program.

Dan became too controlling; he hounded Sipowicz. Dan evaluated his every move. We saw it clearly when he tried to make the decision for Sipowicz about whether Sipowicz should become romantically involved with Sylvia. Dan was unwittingly trying to teach Sipowicz a lesson in psychoanalysis: delay in gratification. He tried to teach Sipowicz to control his "Id." "Wait, don't let yourself get too involved in a love relationship right now," he seemed to be telling Sipowicz. "If you let yourself cave in to your desires for love and sex, you'll soon be seduced back into your desire to drink."

A further example was the "contract" Sipowicz allegedly formed with Dan, a contract regarding control. Apparently Sipowicz had agreed to do what Dan told him to do. It's interesting that Dan was a former cop; now he had become a bit of a spiritual cop. In the episode entitled "For

Whom the Skel Rolls," we saw sponsor Dan once again in the role of dictator. "Nothing is more important than your sobriety," he reminded Sipowicz. That is a potent command: that means your integrity, your job, your family, your love, your health, etc., are less important than your sobriety. In other words, Dan, as sponsor, had assumed the role of the Higher Power. Sipowicz had made a contract with God "as he understood Him." I don't think he bargained for this, and Sipowicz's doubt began to show. He began to suspect that Dan was projecting his own insecurities onto him. In psychoanalysis this is known as "transference."

Sipowicz showed symptoms of skepticism early in the season. He knew he shouldn't drink, and likely bought into a good portion of the "disease model." However, he also knew there was something wrong with Dan's sponsorship. And Sipowicz never really impresses us as a particularly religious person, even when he is forced to deal with terrible misfortune. The fact of the matter is, Sipowicz was controlling his drinking. He seemed to recognize that resisting temptation was within his power. This would be a good indication that he was well on the road to recovery. But AA sees any sense of self-empowerment as "stinkin' thinkin'"—doubting the dogma is dangerous. It will lead inevitably to a fall.

A Totemic Religion

As anthropologist Paul Antze explains it, AA is a totemic religion. A totem "is an animal, plant or natural object serving among certain primitive peoples as the emblem of a clan or family by virtue of an asserted ancestral relationship" (*American Heritage Dictionary*, 1969). Alcohol is a venerated symbol in AA.

Our view of alcohol has changed over time. During Colonial days in America, alcohol was called the "good creature of God." Its use was encouraged by physicians and ministers alike. Trouble that arose from drunkenness then came to be blamed on the tavern one frequented and on the company one kept. But during the alcohol temperance era, alcohol was known as "that engine of the devil." Trouble that arose from drunkenness was then blamed on the substance itself. Alcohol was viewed as a universally addicting substance (Levine, 1978).

In AA thinking, alcohol has a Janus nature. Alcohol is seen as both God and the Devil. It is the Devil in that ingesting the beverage is believed to release a spiritual disease that causes a fall from grace, a descent into hell. But once the religious conversion takes place, once the person abdicates his life to belief in a Higher Power, we see that alcohol in fact is a vehicle to know God. Alcohol thus inspirits and inspires the alcoholic. It helps him to move from "not-God" to God. The alcoholic is inspired to climb a symbolic Jacob's Ladder—the Twelve Steps—and overcome the "pride problem." The pride problem is the true spiritual disease. It just manifests itself through drunkenness.

What we also see here is that alcoholics are "marked"—they are a chosen people according to their ideology—and it is their affliction or wound that not only binds them together, it delivers them to God. The dual symbolic nature of alcohol-as-totem both binds alcoholics together and delivers them to heaven.

A Sisyphean Journey

But AA's views on destructive drinking are not shared by everyone, particularly those in academia who study and write about drinking behavior. Academics debate whether addiction is a choice or a disease. Despite the dominance of the AA position (and its adoption by the *NYPD Blue* writers), there are sharp differences of opinion among experts and laypersons alike as to why people drink—and don't drink—the way they do.

AA has helped many people, and its approach is certainly valid for its adherents. But there are contradictions in its belief structure, as Sipowicz begins to note.

Why, for example, if the pride problem was the true reason why people like Sipowicz drink, shouldn't Sipowicz be able to drink responsibly if he overcame the pride problem? When I have asked old timers this question they always say "no," the alcoholic can never drink again. "But you say they can overcome the pride problem, by working the steps. If the pride problem is the real reason they drink, if thinking that they're God is the real reason they drink, and knowing that they are not God is the real cure, then why can't they drink again?" I keep asking. "Because they are sick," is always the answer.

This is what I think Sipowicz sensed, the circular logic of AA. I don't know what the scriptwriters will do with Sipowicz, but if this were real life, I would predict that a person like Sipowicz would probably evolve to the point where he could take a drink occasionally without losing control.

Certainly the science bears this out. Considerable research exists that indicates that heavy drinking is better explained by mindset, values and interaction with one's environment, rather than genetics, biology and the chemical properties of the drug. In fact, one criticism of AA is that leading people to believe they are predestined to become alcoholics creates a self-fulfilling prophecy.

As noted, there is strong disagreement in the addiction field today—which includes views about alcoholism—as to whether addiction is a disease or a behavior. For many years, conventional wisdom held that alcoholism is a genetic disease characterized by "loss of control." This meant that some people are born to drink alcoholically and thus must abstain from alcohol in its entirety. The idea that an alcoholic could control his or her drinking, that is, learn to drink in moderation, was and continues to be considered anathema by many in treatment and self-help fields.

But since at least the 1960s, scientific research on alcoholism and other addictions has shifted this view. Many alcoholics do learn to drink in moderation—and they do this on their own or with the help of others. In the United Kingdom, Canada and Australia, for example, "controlled-drinking" programs are implemented by treatment providers along with abstinence-oriented ones. In the United States, we're still a bit behind the times. In my book, *Addiction Is a Choice* (Open Court Publishing, 2000), I document the extensive studies showing that alcoholics can control their drinking, when it is important enough to them to do so.

AA has long held that alcoholism is a disease, and AA has long been considered the most effective way of helping people we label as alcoholic. However, scientific research shows that AA is no more effective than other forms of treatment that eschew "the disease model," such as cognitive behavioral therapy and motivational enhancement therapy. Interestingly, studies seem to indicate alcoholics who attempt to quit on their own do as well as those entering structured programs of any kind.

This is important information because many people who need help with alcohol do not like the religious nature of AA, or they are looking for a way to moderate but not abstain from drinking. Alcoholics constitute a heterogeneous population. Everyone drinks in different ways, for different reasons and with different results. Treatment approaches should be similarly diverse. No one shoe fits all.

So will we soon see Sipowicz happily and safely taking a few drinks with his fellow cops? I seriously doubt it.... *NYPD Blue* seems too heavily invested in the AA model of alcoholism. But many real-life Sipowiczs have managed to control their drinking, and who knows, maybe by the series finale Sipowicz will as well.

References

Antze, P. (1987). Symbolic action in Alcoholics Anonymous. In M. Douglas (Ed.) *Constructive Drinking: Perspectives on Drink from Anthropology* (New York: Cambridge University Press) 149–181.

Greil, A.L. and Rudy, D.R. (1983). Conversion to the world view of Alcoholics Anonymous: A refinement of conversion theory. *Qualitative Sociology* 6: 5–28.

Kurtz, E. (1988). *A.A.: The Story* (A revised edition of *Not God: A History of Alcoholics Anonymous*). (New York: Harper & Row).

Levine, H.G. (1978). The discovery of addiction. *Journal of Studies on Alcohol* 39: 143–174.

Morris, W. (Ed.) (1969). *The American Heritage Dictionary of the English Language*. (Boston: American Heritage Publishing Co., Inc. and Houghton Mifflin Company).

Sessions, P. M. (1957). Ego religion and superego religion in alcoholics. *Quarterly Journal of Studies on Alcohol* 18: 121–125.

Stewart, D.A. (1954). The dynamics of fellowship as illustrated in Alcoholics Anonymous. *Quarterly Journal of Studies on Alcohol* 16: 251–262.

Jeffrey Schaler, Ph.D., a psychologist, is assistant professor of justice, law and society at American University's School of Public Affairs in Washington, D.C. He is the author of Addiction Is a Choice *(2000) and editor of* Szasz Under Fire: The Psychiatric Abolitionist Faces His Critics *(2004), both published by Open Court Publishing Company, Chicago.*

DAVID GERROLD

In Search
of Blanche Dubois

*David Gerrold is one of my heroes. He wrote—while in col-
lege!—"The Trouble With Tribbles," an episode of* Star Trek *selected by fans as the best of the series. He's written countless
award-winning novels, including one of the truly great works
of science fiction,* The Man Who Folded Himself. *In addition
to being the best time travel novel ever written,* The Man Who
Folded Himself *was one of the first science fiction novels with a
gay hero. In this essay Gerrold looks at television, homosexuality, gay John and "Blanche Dubois."*

L ET'S START WITH *Hill Street Blues.*
That's where Steven Bochco first reinvented the cop show.
Prior to *Hill Street Blues,* cop shows were usually variations on
Dragnet: interview the victims, run some license plates, interview some
witnesses, take some fingerprints, interview the suspects, put all the
pieces together, chase someone (optional) and conclude with an arrest.
Of course, from the perspective of the cop show, the suspect was pre-
sumed guilty; the police don't arrest innocent people.

This perception of police authority began to shift in 1966, when the
Supreme Court heard the case of *Miranda v. Arizona,* and overturned
the conviction of one Ernesto Miranda who had confessed to a crime
without knowing he had the right to an attorney. Miranda was guilty of

the crime, but the system, as it was structured, had failed to respect his rights as a citizen. After 1966, television arrests included reading the suspect his rights, i.e. *mirandizing* him: "You have the right to remain silent. Anything you say can and will be used against you in a court of law. You have the right to speak to an attorney, and to have an attorney present during any questioning. If you cannot afford a lawyer, one will be provided for you at government expense."

But unlike real life, the last act of any cop show, whether it is the original *Dragnet* or the more contemporary *CSI*, usually involves the perpetrator explaining why he did it and the arresting officer, the hero of the show, putting the punch line on the scene as well as the show: some variation of "You're not only wrong, you're a stupid asshole."

Television isn't about real life; it's a convenient shorthand for real life. At best, it's a fractured mirror of what television producers think real life is. A television drama starts with the problem to be solved—there's been a robbery, a rape, a murder. The job of the detectives is to solve the problem; therefore, when the perpetrator is apprehended, the problem is solved. Hence, the assumption that the perp is not only guilty—because our heroes always get the right guy—but also that he's a stupid asshole for breaking the law in the first place. And if he's hurt, injured, raped or killed someone in the process, well then, he's not really entitled to much sympathy or understanding, is he? That part of cop shows hasn't changed.

Hill Street Blues premiered in January of 1981; NBC ran the first episode on Thursday, January 15, and the second episode two nights later. The following week, they did it again, running the third episode on Thursday and the fourth on Saturday. (After that, the show aired regularly on Saturday evenings.) This was an unheard of programming stunt for introducing a new series.

But it introduced audiences to the concept of a series that told its stories in multipart arcs; it also made it possible for the late-arriving audience to catch up and get involved with the show a lot faster.

Hill Street Blues had an ensemble cast, running through multiple interwoven, multipart storylines. Where most television series are content to have three storylines, an "A-line" (the main story), a "B-line" (the secondary story) and a "C-line" (an unimportant subplot) with everything resolving in the last five minutes, *Hill Street Blues* usually juggled as many as five or six separate storylines, all with varying degrees of importance, stretching out over several weeks. The pace was frenetic and exciting.

Nevertheless, as a mid-season replacement, the show was competing against established viewing habits; despite heavy promotion from the network, the series languished in the ratings.

At the end of March, after running the first thirteen episodes, the network replayed the first two episodes back-to-back. A week later it played episodes three and four back-to-back, specifically advertising to all those viewers who had missed the premiere: "Now you can see it from the beginning!" This led off six weeks of repeats. Viewers who had originally passed on what they thought was "just another cop show," but who had since read the great reviews, or heard from friends how good the show was, tuned in for a look-see. After airing two two-hour episodes in May, NBC repeated the entire first season again, during the summer.

Then, in September *Hill Street Blues* was nominated for a record number of Emmy awards. Five weeks later, the show took home trophies for writing, directing, lead actor and actress, supporting actor and outstanding drama series. It also won two technical awards. *Hill Street Blues* won more Emmys in its premiere season than any other television series in the history of the awards, a record that still has not been broken. This critical recognition finally propelled the series into the ranks of the top ten rated shows.

Hill Street Blues was certainly influenced by movies like *The French Connection* (1971) and *Serpico* (1973). It didn't look like any other TV show before it. The flavor was gritty and hard, the camera work was fluid, the characters were realistic and often obnoxious, and the characters' language had outright vulgarities and often flirted with obscene entendres. (Lt. Howard Hunter, played by James B. Sikking, would say things like, "Frank, I'll be dipped in brown sauce before I'll...etc.") There was a savage streak of black comedy throughout. Clearly the writers were pushing the limits. The storytelling was multilayered, convoluted and accelerated to a remarkable pace. You had to actually *watch* this show—you couldn't go off and do the dishes and listen from the other room.

Most important, the cops on the hill were seen as a variety of types, from admirable to offensive, and the surrounding community wasn't much better. These people had lives; they didn't chitchat over doughnuts, they got down and wallowed in the moment-to-moment angst of their problems. They *hurt*.

We were never shown which city the series existed in—it used Los Angeles locations, but had an East Coast flavor. It could have been any major American metropolis with underpaid, overworked cops working a black ghetto with whores, junkies, con men and car thieves.

Very quickly familiar moments and running gags began to develop. Almost every show began with a morning briefing, which always concluded with Sgt. Phil Esterhaus saying, "Lets be careful out there."

Det. Mick Belker, played by Bruce Weitz, had the look and manner of a scruffy, half-starved, rabid coyote; he arrested perps by screaming and leaping. He'd drag them into the station house with terms of endearment like "dog-breath" and unfettered admonitions: "One more word and I'll rip your lungs out through your nose." Belker would sit the collar down next to his desk, roll an arrest form into his battered old typewriter and ask, "Name...?" Sometimes, before the perp could answer, Belker's phone would ring. Answering it, his manner would change, soften and he'd say, "Hello, Ma...." Belker's unseen mother was another running gag. And oftentimes, after finishing the conversation—"I gotta go, Ma, I got work to do"—he'd look across to see the arrestee's bemused expression. This usually earned the perp a quick, "What're you looking at, hair-bag?"

Several of these perps became running gags in themselves, like the bald-headed pickpocket. One of the best was a gay male prostitute played by Charles Levin; the first time he appeared, Belker dragged him in and sat him down, rolling a form into the typewriter, and asked, "Name?" The character was unapologetically gay. He smiled across at Belker and said innocently: "Dubois. Blanche Dubois." End of scene. Cut to commercial while the more knowledgeable members of the audience howl in glee.

Okay, that joke might not be immediately obvious to the average viewer. You have to be literate. In fact, you have to be gay-literate to get it. But it reveals the depth of the writers' reach. Blanche Dubois is Stella's deranged sister in *A Streetcar Named Desire*, generally regarded as Tennessee Williams' best play. Blanche is famous for what may be the most immortal epitaph in theater history; at the end of the play, as she is being led away by the doctors, she says, "Whoever you are, I have always depended on the kindness of strangers." The line is both tragic and funny—Williams himself said he always thought of that line as a joke. But it has also become gay camp, in much the same vein as, "Fasten your seat belts, it's going to be a bumpy night" (Bette Davis as Margo Channing, *All About Eve*), or "You have no power here! Begone, before somebody drops a house on you too!" (Billie Burke as Glinda the Good Witch of the North, *The Wizard of Oz*.)

More important, this character—Eddie Gregg—was one of the first recurring portrayals of a gay man in a prime-time dramatic series. Eddie Gregg appeared in the first episode of the 1982–83 season, "Trial by Fury" (September 30, 1982), as well as four episodes after that, eventually becoming a snitch for Belker in "A Hair of the Dog." In the following episode, "Phantom of the Hill," a terrified Eddie Gregg implicated his lover in the violent murders of a group of Peruvian drug dealers.

Prior to this, gay characters had been seen primarily in sitcoms, and almost always for the comedic discomfort of one of the show's leads; most notably Archie Bunker (Carroll O'Connor) in *All in the Family,* or Phyllis (Cloris Leachman) on *The Mary Tyler Moore Show.* Archie was dismayed to find out that the female passenger to whom he'd given mouth-to-mouth resuscitation was really a man; Phyllis was relieved to find out that her brother was gay rather than have him dating the very Jewish Rhoda. Other than the occasional British miniseries like *Brideshead Revisited* or *Tinker, Tailor, Soldier, Spy*, gay people didn't really exist on television.

For the longest time, television's only acknowledgment of gay men and lesbians was as outsiders, freaks, fringe-dwellers—objects of patronizing tolerance or cheap jokes based on discomfort and embarrassment. (This, at least, was moderately better than the way gay people were portrayed in the movies; to a great degree, if gay characters were included at all, they were portrayed either as killers or creeps or victims, usually destined for a brutal end, usually suicide—because obviously the shame of being homosexual was just too much for anyone to live with.) In the mid-eighties, this started to change; if a gay man appeared on a prime-time television drama, he was dying of AIDS or watching his lover die of the disease.

The real shift in perception actually began in 1969. (Television has always been a a half-step behind.) Judy Garland died on June 22, 1969. Coincidentally—or maybe *not* coincidentally—that same day, there was a tornado in Kansas. Her funeral was held on Friday, June 27, at the Frank E. Campbell funeral home at Madison Avenue and Eighty-first Street in Manhattan. Twenty-two thousand people filed past Judy's open coffin over a twenty-four-hour period. Her ex-husband, Vincent Minnelli did not attend. James Mason, her costar in the 1954 version of *A Star Is Born*, delivered the eulogy.

That evening, a crowd of drag queens gathered for a private wake of their own at the Stonewall Inn, an inconspicuous hole in the wall on Christopher Street, just a short distance north of Seventh Avenue. That *same* evening, not realizing what they were walking into (and probably not caring anyway), police officers and agents of the Alcoholic Beverage Control Board raided the place, ostensibly to look for violations. As they had done many times before, they insulted and abused the patrons with homophobic remarks; they checked IDs, then ejected the men one-by-one from the bar.

But on this evening, angered by the invasion of their own memorial to Judy, the drag queens didn't disappear into the night. They gathered out front—joined by hustlers, students, neighborhood residents and curious cruisers—and released years of smoldering resentment. *The drag queens fought back.*[2] Someone uprooted a parking meter and used it to barricade the door, trapping the police and ABC agents inside the bar. Reinforcements arrived with screaming sirens and flashing lights. So, of course, the crowd grew. What started out as a routine harassment of the patrons of a gay bar had suddenly turned into a riot. And the rioters were suddenly chanting, "Gay Power! Gay Power!"

The next evening an impromptu street carnival started up in front of the bar, celebrating the previous night's events. But the police, unamused by their own public embarrassment, were out in force, determined not to have a repeat performance; they lined up across the street from the bar, wearing visors and carrying batons, and moved into the crowd—the crowd fought back. And the riot began again. Monday and Tuesday, it rained. Wednesday saw a mini-riot, though relatively subdued by the standards of the weekend.

This wasn't the first time that gay people had resisted an abuse of police power. Eight months earlier, police had raided a leather bar in the Silverlake district of Los Angeles and triggered a mini-riot there. As later events would clearly demonstrate, there was growing gay resentment toward the police and their deliberate harassment of gay men and lesbians, but Stonewall was the first time that such resistance made the national news—radio, television, newspapers—and it took on mythic significance. It electrified gay people all across the country.

In the months that followed, five separate gay liberation fronts sprang up in New York, Berkeley, Los Angeles, San Francisco and San Jose. By the end of 1970, three hundred gay liberation fronts had been formed nationwide. A commemoration of the Stonewall Rebellion was held in August, 1969, and marches were held in 1970 in New York and Los Angeles on the anniversary. Since then, Gay Pride Day and Gay Pride

---

[2] Shakespeare had it wrong. Hell hath no fury like a drag queen.

Week have become annual celebrations in most major American cities, usually (but not always) held on the anniversary of the Stonewall uprising. Today, a plaque can be found on the wall outside of the Stonewall Inn, commemorating the revolution.

But the real revolution for gay people was a revolution of *self*.

For the first few years, much of the gay liberation movement was about defining the gay liberation movement and what it meant to be gay. That was an exhausting deadend; ultimately, gay people began to realize that there were as many different kinds of gay people as there were people, and each person was inventing "gay" in his or her own way. That acceptance of diversity was the beginning of a real gay community. That was the beginning of gay self-definition.

Prior to Stonewall, gay identity had been defined by straight people. Straight legislators had defined homosexuality as a crime. Straight doctors had defined it as a sickness. Straight psychiatrists had defined it as a disorder. Straight theologians defined homosexuality as a sin. Straight ministers defined it as immoral. The Catholic Church said it was about child molesting....

Okay, time for a quick quiz. What's wrong with this picture? Right. It's straight people pretending to be experts on what it is to be gay. This is as silly as white people explaining to black people what it means to be black. How long do you think black people would put up with that?

The astonishing irony of this situation is that when gay people finally did begin to speak out that these definitions were unfair, many straight people replied that gay people were obviously too biased to have credible opinions. To the gay community, that sounded like: "Shut up. We'll tell you who and what you are. You're the people my mother warned me about. You're not deserving of respect." The idea that there might be a straight bias did not occur to these folks.

Ultimately, there was only one way for gay men and lesbians to respond: with confrontation—both polite and otherwise. Every lie repeated by a bigot became an opportunity for rebuttal—an invitation to bring out the truth. That's what Stonewall unleashed: a long-overdue scream of outrage by a group of people who had not yet had the chance to find out who they really were—and who were inventing it now. This was a moment of transformation—gay people were finally taking ownership of their own identities. The gay pride parades became a celebration of the myriad different ways of being gay. Contingents of gay lawyers, gay doctors, gay students, gay Latinos, gay blacks, gay Asians, gay social workers, dykes on bykes, gym-bunnies, gay parents, gay seniors and yes, of course, lots of drag queens, all became familiar participants in marches all across the country; but the folks who always garner the greatest applause are P-FLAG, the Parents and Friends of Lesbians and Gays—the families who openly support their gay children.

Like Glinda the Good urging the Munchkins to "Come out, come out, wherever you are," activists within the gay community continued to urge gay people everywhere to come out of their closets and be known to their friends and families and coworkers. As difficult as that process might seem from inside the closet, once the step was taken it was also profoundly liberating—not only on a personal level, but on a social level as well. The public visibility of gay people, both as individuals and as a community, was the most direct and effective way for gay people to tell the larger community of straights: "No. You do not tell us who we are. *We will tell you* who we are." By being visible, by being public, by being openly out and gay—by being *unashamed*—gay people demonstrated that they were defining their own identity.

One of the major battlegrounds has always been the media—the channels of information that shape public perception of people and events. The Gay and Lesbian Alliance Against Defamation (GLAAD) wasn't formed until 1985. Before that, the gay community didn't have a media watchdog.

Nevertheless, many people working in television were beginning to get the message. Spurred by the growing visibility of gay men and lesbians in public life, more and more shows began to include gay characters and storylines; but the appearance of Eddie Gregg on *Hill Street Blues* is noteworthy precisely because once he had a name, once he was no longer "Blanche Dubois," Eddie Gregg became a very real character—no longer a convenient stereotype, no longer the butt of the joke. It was a start.

Eddie Gregg returned to the hill for one final appearance, ("Slum Enchanted Evening") in the 1985—86 season. He was losing his battle with AIDS, helping to fuel a crisis of confidence for Belker, who was beginning to fear that he couldn't get close to anybody, because if he did, they would die. But even more importantly, Eddie Gregg's death helped to put a human face on the headlines, helping to make real the growing AIDS crisis that many Americans still did not understand.

After *Hill Street Blues*, Steven Bochco created *L.A. Law*, another series which depended on an ensemble cast and multiple storylines. This time, the focus was a well-established law firm in downtown Los Angeles. The show was an immediate hit, running for eight years (1986–1994) and even inspiring a reunion made-for-TV movie in 2003.

Because the show focused primarily on the cases and the clients, *L.A. Law* was strongly issue-oriented. Over the years, it had several episodes involving gay issues, usually with insight and compassion. One episode in particular, "Do The Spike Thing" (1991), began with Senior Partner Douglas Brachman (this series' equivalent of *Hill Street Blues*' obnoxious-but-inwardly-sensitive Lt. Howard Hunter) having dinner with DA Robert Caporale. Caporale and Brachman were old friends; we'd previously seen Caporale in the 1987 episode "Pigmalion."

In the course of the dinner, Caporale told Brachman that he was gay. After Brachman's initial discomfort, Caporale asked him to be the best man at his upcoming wedding. (This was in 1991, a time when same-sex marriage was a commitment ceremony without legal recognition, long before the complex history of real-world legal and political wrangles even began.) Caporale was played by Charles Levin, the same actor who played Eddie Gregg on *Hill Street Blues*.

After leaving the restaurant, Brachman was assaulted by a gay-basher. Even though the assailant was caught, Brachman was reluctant to testify against him, because he did not want anyone to misunderstand and think he himself was gay. Ultimately, however—after Caporale implied to his face that he was both a coward and a hypocrite—Brachman found whatever it was he used for courage and testified. When asked if he was straight or gay, he replied that his sexual orientation was irrelevant to the issue. While not exactly a believable answer, it was the necessary sermon for this subplot.

The real point here is that even though Charles Levin's part was a relatively small one, the kind of character he played represented a dramatic shift in perception. He was no longer portraying a gay man as a prostitute and a snitch—now he was a district attorney planning a same-sex commitment ceremony. Through Steven Bochco and other producers with integrity, television was working its way toward a grudging acceptance of equality.

After *L.A. Law*, Bochco produced the short-lived *Cop Rock* (apparently I was the only person in North America who actually liked this show), *Hooperman* and *Doogie Howser*. But in 1993, Bochco returned to the streets with *NYPD Blue*, starring Dennis Franz as Det. Andy Sipowicz.

From the beginning *NYPD Blue* pushed the boundaries of what was possible on American television, including the use of words like "asshole" and "prick" and a frightening nude shot of Dennis Franz's naked butt. The earliest episodes had camerawork so liquid it was dizzying, but this particular aspect of the show calmed down with time, as the producers and directors developed the look and feel of the series.

Unlike *Hill Street Blues* and *L.A. Law*, *NYPD Blue* is not an ensemble show. It focuses instead on the character and casework of Andy Sipowicz, a scruffy boulder of a man with a scowl that cuts ice. Sipowicz is as far removed from *Hill Street's* Frank Furillo as Furillo was from *Dragnet's* Sgt. Joe Friday. Sipowicz is rough-hewn and almost deliberately unlikable. He is a purpose-driven force of nature and has all the subtlety of an earthquake. This is not a man who has time for bullshit.

Andy Sipowicz operates at street-level; in his worldview the ends justify the means, especially if he's out of time or patience. If necessary, he will push an uncooperative witness into the wall, he will cock his fist inches from a perpetrator's face and physically threaten him. He is—to be blunt—a terrifying cop. He is not a man you want knocking on your door and announcing, "Police, open up."

During the course of the show, Sipowicz has gone through a succession of partners, played in turn by David Caruso (formerly "Shamrock," the leader of the Irish gang on *Hill Street Blues*), Jimmy Smits (formerly of *L.A. Law*) and Rick Schroeder, all of whom left the series to pursue other concerns. Men come and go, but Sipowicz abides. He may be bloodied, but he remains unbowed. He has mellowed somewhat—getting married does that to a television hero—but he hasn't lost his ability to bite, chew and spit.

In many ways, the character of Sipowicz is the *point* of the series. Andy Sipowicz is the living demonstration of the cost. He's been on the front lines of the war zone most of his life and the battle scars are visible in his eyes, in his heavy posture, in the way he moves through the terrible weight of the job. Sipowicz bears silent witness; he doesn't have to speak, it's written in his reactions, his knowing expressions.

NYPD Blue is not the hill. Not in tone, not in intention, not in focus. Unlike *Hill Street Blues*, the focus is not on the cases as much as it is on how the cases affect the detectives who have to deal with them. It's about how law enforcement is influenced by personal issues—the detective who has already dealt with his drinking problem is quick to recognize when another detective is headed down the same destructive path. The detective who failed to call for early intervention when his own father needed it worries if he should turn in an officer showing stress. Sometimes it seems as if cases occur specifically to dredge up pieces of the inescapable past. Yes, of course, they do—that's exactly how television drama works. The story is about testing the hero, over and over and over again.

Television isn't about accurately portraying the world—it's about reflecting it. The image is refracted through the opinions of producers, writers, directors, actors and everyone else who gets a voice in the production. A television show is a recreation, a simulation, an evocation of time and place and spirit. It's a shorthand view of life.

One network executive (it may have been Fred Silverman) once said that American television isn't about leading the way, it's about staying safely one half-step behind. But that's not quite accurate. Television comes from the coasts, from New York and Los Angeles. Middle America is "the people we fly over." Television comes from rich white guys who live in New York and Los Angeles, who look around and see what's happening in their neighborhoods and write it into their shows. So, if it's true that most social trends start on the coasts and work their way inward, then television, which might be a half-step behind the coasts, is still a full step ahead of the heartland.

For much of the country, prime-time television drama is dragging, pushing, propelling them headlong into greater awareness of things that make them uncomfortable. There's a resentment there, which has always been there; it's the cultural gap. It's the fear of the unknown and the annoyance of having to deal with it. This is nowhere so true as with the growing awareness of the role of gay people in the national arena.

When prime-time drama first became issue-oriented in the late-sixties, early seventies, it was considered *important* for a show to be relevant. That was the key word—relevancy. So stories were derived not simply from events found on the front pages, but also on the issues behind those events. And as fast as television puts these issues on the air, makes them topics of common conversation, attitudes shift and change and evolve.

Today, almost all of the major prime-time shows are dealing with human issues with a degree of realism unimaginable even a decade ago. The reactions of Douglas Brachman to gay issues in the 1991 episode of *L.A. Law* ("Do The Spike Thing") look quaint by current cultural standards.

Sometimes producers lose a sense of perspective. Sometimes they miss the point entirely. One recent cop show dealt with the issue of hate crimes. The detectives were tracking down two men who had assaulted two gay men and killed one of them. It turned out that the argument was over a parking space, not over the victims' sexuality. Fair enough. That's a good issue to raise—when is a hate crime not a hate crime? But as the episode progressed, every single officer on the team made a point of saying (almost bragging?) that he or she had a gay relative or friend, thus indicating his or her inherent sympathy for gay people. (Right. "Some of my best friends are queers." Hello, it's 2004—don't you folks get it how stupid that sounds?)

In that same show, the DA who intended to prosecute the case as a hate crime anyway, was also a lesbian mother. The implication here is that gay people have become so overzealous in prosecuting hate crimes that we must prosecute *any* crime against gay people as an act of bias. Even that might not be a bad issue to raise, but…the punch line of the episode had one of the older officers asking a younger one what she thought of the case. This was it—*the speech.*[3] What did she say? She said, "Aren't all crimes really hate crimes? Don't you have to make it up in your head that you hate someone in order to commit a crime against them?"

Aaarrrrrggghhhh!!!

Obviously, the producers of this show had no idea just how frustrating and obnoxious that particular "speech" would be to gay viewers. It is exactly the argument that homophobes and bigots and ignorant legislators have made specifically to *resist* the enactment of hate crime laws. It's simplistic. It's an easy rationalization. *And it's wrong.* Because all crimes are *not* hate crimes. The mugger who goes for your wallet—he's not interested in who you sleep with; he just wants your money. As soon as he gets it, he's gone. That's not hate; it's greed and desperation. The car thief who carjacks your Honda drives it off to a chop-shop for parts—he doesn't care who you come home to in the evening; he just wants the car and the money he'll make off of it. As soon as he gets the car, he's gone.

But the gay-basher, the guy who beats you up with a baseball bat, all the time shouting, "Die, you stinking queer!"—he's not interested in your wallet or your car; he's going for the emotional payoff. And he won't stop, can't stop, until he's both physically and emotionally exhausted. Hate crimes are defined by the motive of the perpetrator—and the motive is knowable by what he says and does. Shouting, "Die, faggot, die!" is usually a pretty good indicator of a perpetrator's intentions. Compared to all other assaults, hate crimes are the most vicious, the most deadly and the most injurious to the victims. There is a difference—and real cops know and understand it. The producers of that

---

[3] The speech is that moment at the end of a movie or TV show when the hero delivers his or her moral judgment on the whole affair. James T. Kirk often had many of the best speeches: "Yes, I'm descended from killer apes. But today, I'm not going to kill." And, "Let's get the hell out of here." (Ask a Trekkie.)

above-mentioned show didn't, but real cops who arrive on the scene while the blood is still flowing warm on the pavement—they know, because they've seen it.

That's why *NYPD Blue* works so well. Because its people are simply people.

The show doesn't try to explain the world, doesn't offer a grand moral point of view, doesn't preach—the characters simply try to survive as well as they can and scrabble out a bit of personal peace, something everybody can relate to.

Ironically, despite his demeanor, Andy Sipowicz is the Zen master of the show. He looks world-weary, but underlying that he demonstrates a clear acceptance of the chaotic nature of life. He gets it—he understands that each of us chooses his or her own way. From that essential insight, he has distilled a remarkably pragmatic attitude toward others. If they're making a difference, they're okay. If they're sick or injured or hurt, they need help. If they're hurting others, they have to be stopped—by whatever means available. It's a simplistic moral compass, to be sure, but it's incredibly accurate. At the end of an episode, Sipowicz doesn't give *the speech*. He gives a scowl, or a shrug or even occasionally a small, but honest, piece of himself. How can you not fall in love with this man?

One thing about people on TV: whether we do it consciously or not, we use them as role models. (Need proof? Remember everybody saying, "Whaaaaazzzzuppp?" to everybody else for several annoying months?) This is why television represents a primary avenue of social transformation. Television not only tracks social changes, it facilitates them. Other minorities and ethnicities have seen this: blacks, Latinos, Asians, the disabled, the elderly and especially women. Steven Bochco's shows have been a large part of this process.

As minorities have become a presence on television, what changes isn't just their portrayal, but also how others regard them. There are several steps: first they are objects of ridicule; then victims deserving patronizing tolerance; then guest stars who have the right to explain, justify and defend themselves; then sidekicks and occasionally partners; and ultimately, finally, heroes in their own right. This is the path that blacks and Latinos have traveled; it's the same path that gay people are on.

But it's not simply the portrayal of gay people that's essential here—it's also the way that the straight characters, especially the heroes of the series, treat the gay characters in their regular interactions. Because that's the role model for the folks at home watching the show.

Here's one of the litmus tests—if a gay character is portrayed, is his homosexuality the issue? What is everybody else in the story talking about? If the character's homosexuality is incidental to the primary issue of the story, that's a sign of acceptance; but if the character's homosexuality is simply the jumping off point for another variation of "queers are people too," then perhaps somebody is trying to salve his conscience.

From the very first season, *NYPD Blue* has included the character of John Irvin, a receptionist/assistant, openly and recognizably "of the gay persuasion." Played by Bill Brochtrup, "gay John" is the fluttery blond guy who passes phone messages and runs minor errands. Is he stereotypical or not? Opinions vary, but the character is generally treated with respect and compassion. Occasionally, his homosexuality has been used as a springboard for a storyline.

In the 1995 episode "The Bank Dick" (apparently mistitled, it had nothing to do with either banks or dicks), John asked Bobby Simone (Jimmy Smits) for help. He and his new boyfriend were gay-bashed; neither were seriously harmed. The boyfriend was Paul Caputo, a closeted officer in another precinct. The gay-bashers were two black teenagers hired by other officers in Caputo's precinct who found out Caputo's secret. This was a "C-story," a very small subplot tucked in between several other running stories. Simone met with Caputo and offered him advice; Caputo insisted that he would handle the situation his own way. Simone then met with the two officers who hired the gay-bashers and told them if anything else happened to Caputo, he'd have them up before the Internal Affairs Division. Later, Caputo confronted Simone; he didn't want Simone to get involved. Simone said, "I didn't want you doing anything stupid." Then we got to *the speech*, where Simone advised Caputo that sooner or later, he was going to have to come to terms with his situation; i.e. come out of the closet. Later "gay John" told Simone that Caputo was seeing a counselor. And once again, the wise straight person solved the gay problem.

This subplot may be compassionate in its intentions, but on one level it represents an essential failure of understanding. It is a straight man advising a gay man on how to behave. It's also an example of what some gay critics call "colonization of the issue"—what happens when those of the "straight-but-sensitive" persuasion adopt an issue to demonstrate their enlightenment. So here we have a straight man arguing for a gay man's self-acceptance. This establishes that Simone not only "gets it," but that because he's a positive role model, other open-minded straight people get it too.

Well, yes, okay, fine—but for gay viewers, this was just another straight person speaking when he should be listening. The person making the speech shouldn't have been Bobby Simone, but "gay John." And in fact, there's another speech "gay John" should have made to Detective Simone: it is impossible for any straight person to truly understand the closet and the fear of coming out, because he hasn't lived it.

There's an old joke about the difference between being black and gay. If you're black, you don't have to tell your momma. The joke isn't just funny, it's also tragic. Almost all gay people have heterosexual parents. The gay teen, realizing his or her homosexuality, also realizes he or she is *different*—not just different from friends and neighbors, but different from his or her parents as well. This produces a feeling of alienation; even in the most loving of homes there's a period of distancing. The teen becomes anxious, reluctant, fearful, even desperate—because what if Mom and Dad can't understand? Adolescence is already a period of extraordinary angst—that's when you discover your ability to be truly depressed. The emotional foundation for a teenager's well-being is created by mom and dad, so the possibility of rejection on any level is terrifying. Coming out isn't simply about saying to folks, "Hey, I'm gay." It is about dealing with their reactions. And unfortunately, because there is still so much misinformation and misunderstanding of homosexuality, many parents take the news badly; they make it about themselves: "What did we do wrong?" or "How can you do this to us?" (A simple "You're still my son/daughter and I still love you," is much more appropriate—and in some cases, lifesaving.)

That's the real issue that a gay person faces in coming out—dealing with the possibility of rejection from those you love the most. That's the big barrier. No other minority group has to deal with that issue as part of its cultural identity. And although many television shows, movies, books and plays have addressed this moment, sometimes it seems as if the straight world still has trouble wrapping its head around the idea that coming out isn't an admission of something awful, it's actually a moment of self-liberation, it is an act of celebration. (One day, I'd like to see the following dialogue in a TV episode: "Mom, Dad, I'm gay." "Oh, thank God. We were afraid we'd have to tell you.")

What would have helped the above episode? Perhaps just a couple of lines of dialogue:

JOHN: You don't understand.
SIMONE: What is it I need to understand here?
JOHN: That you don't understand.

That, at least, would indicate that John, as well as his boyfriend, have some ownership of their own lives; they're not victims, they're experienced in their own world. What they should have been asking for was not a straight man helping gay men, but a straight man taking responsibility for prejudices of other straight people. As a Latino, Simone could then have used that experience as a source of empathy for this story.

The comparison of different prejudices was directly addressed in the 2001 episode "Everyone Into the Poole." In that episode, Medavoy and Jones investigated a robbery-killing of a Chinese restaurant owner by two black teenagers, a girl and a boy; the boy believed that Chinese were parasites, feeding on the black community. To get a confession, Jones didn't tell the teens or their parents that the victim had died; the parent of the boy revealed himself as the source of his son's bigotry against Asians. Later, after the confessions, when the death of the victim was revealed, when Jones told the parents that their children would be arrested, booked and tried for robbery-homicide, the girl's grandmother bawled him out for lying, and the boy's father accused him of betraying black people. In that same episode, Sipowicz and Sorenson investigated the kidnapping of Victor Poole, a gay man, but after they solved the case, he accused them of being homophobic, of allowing their feelings to influence the way they questioned him. Gay John stood up for Sipowicz and Sorenson, but Poole replied, "You don't know what they say behind your back." The camera cut to the other officers in the room, who looked away embarrassed. The point is twofold. Even when you work hard to keep prejudice out of the job, you're still going to be accused. And it stings. But ... it's the right question to ask. Do you still have residual bias coloring your behavior?

To be fair, *NYPD Blue* isn't about gay people, and it has no obligation to be an advocate for any issue, gay or otherwise. That's not the job.

In television, the first commandment is *keep the viewers watching the commercials*. The best way to do that is to entertain the audience. And the best way to entertain the audience is with quality, thought-provoking, character-driven drama. *NYPD Blue* fulfills that obligation. The show is about the long journey of Andy Sipowicz—it's about healing, it's about redemption, it's about rediscovering humanity in the face of massive brutality.

As a cop, Sipowicz isn't going to see a crosssection of any community—he's only going to meet victims, witnesses and perps. And other cops. But even within that limited repertoire of possibility, television drama still has a responsibility to be fair and honest about the people it portrays.

In the real world, the long journey of gay people toward full equality in the national community remains an ongoing trek. For the most part, network television drama still deals with the subject uneasily, relegating gay people to the roles of sidekicks and assistants. Or sometimes as objects of melodrama: Officer Abby Sullivan, played by Paige Turco, ultimately came out as a lesbian; shortly after that she decided to get pregnant (with Medavoy as the sperm donor); then her lover was murdered, she had a baby off-screen and she has since disappeared from the show's radar. Perhaps there's still concern in the executive offices that the "flyover states" won't accept a recurring gay character. If so, it's time to put that concern to rest.

Over on HBO, viewers can see a very matter-of-fact, no-nonsense lesbian officer in the gritty cop series *The Wire*. She's in a committed relationship, and her homosexuality is a non-issue; Shakima Greggs is a fully developed character in her own right. The audience has not only accepted Greggs, they've embraced her as a favorite. Perhaps when Sipowicz exhausts his current partner, John Clark, Jr., Greggs could transfer up from Baltimore....

Meanwhile, Sipowicz continues to evolve. His raised eyebrow still evokes volumes of discontent; but now he's added a few new expressions. One of them almost looks like patience, and the other vaguely resembles compassion. (But I could be wrong about that.)

Oh, one more thing.

Remember Blanche Dubois?

In 1994, Charles Levin appeared in three consecutive episodes of *NYPD Blue*, playing Maury Abrams, Esq., a high-priced lawyer. But not gay.

Too bad. It might have been fun to see one more transformation of Blanche Dubois.

David Gerrold is the author of numerous television episodes including the legendary "Trouble With Tribbles" episode of Star Trek. *He has also written for* Land of the Lost, Babylon 5, Twilight Zone, Sliders *and other series. He has published forty-three books, including two on television production. He taught screenwriting at Pepperdine University for two decades. He has won the Hugo, the Nebula and the Locus award. A movie based on his autobiographical novel,* The Martian Child, *is now in production.*

ROBERT LEONARD

Forensic Linguistics in *NYPD Blue*

NYPD Blue *taught us a new language. We avoid skels in the street, reach out to old friends and try to avoid a jackpot. But* NYPD Blue *teaches us much more than police slang. As forensic linguist Leonard explains,* NYPD Blue *is a window into the complex world of legal language. The uses and misuses of language, in the courtroom and in the interrogation room, can be the difference between success and failure for both the detectives of* NYPD Blue *and the real-life detectives on the streets.*

Setting the Scene

NYPD Blue's tenth season ended with an explosive climax. Captain Fraker of the Internal Affairs Bureau—the hated Rat Squad—had been pursuing a vendetta against the detectives of the 15th Precinct. A special hatred for Rodriguez and Sipowicz consumed him: Fraker claimed Rodriguez ratted him out and that Sipowicz was no better than a blackmailer. Then Fraker's world fell apart—the same day he was passed over for promotion his wife discovered his secret affair with a subordinate cop and threw him out. Drunk as hell, he went to the 15th Precinct, confronted Rodriguez—and shot him point blank.

He raised his gun again, and *bam!* Fraker went down, shot by a trembling Det. Rita Ortiz.

Okay. Rodriguez pulled through. The rat Fraker pulled through. *We know what happened; we* know how evil Fraker is and how unjustified his grudges were. *We* know he shot Rodriguez with no provocation.

In the next season's opener, we found ourselves in court. Fraker was being tried for attempted murder. But things weren't going well. There in court, nothing was as clear as when we saw it go down. Fraker's defense was that Rodriguez drew on *him!* Assistant District Attorney Haywood (Detective Baldwin's on-again-off-again girlfriend, fiancée, almost-mother-of-his-child) had on the stand the emergency room doctor who treated Fraker after Ortiz shot him, Dr. Devlin (Detective Clark's current, very involved girlfriend).

> DR. DEVLIN: Hand-eye coordination would be substantially diminished.
>
> ADA HAYWOOD: So in your opinion, if a man as intoxicated as Captain Fraker saw a sober man draw his own gun, would Captain Fraker be able to outdraw the sober man?
>
> DEFENSE ATTORNEY JAMES SINCLAIR: Objection, speculation—this is a medical witness, not a cowgirl. (jurors laugh, smile at each other)
>
> JUDGE: Sustained.
>
> ADA HAYWOOD: Dr. Devlin, during the course of your treatment of the defendant did he say anything to you?
>
> DR. DEVLIN: He said, "I hope the bastard's dead." He kept repeating that.
>
> ADA HAYWOOD: Thank you.
>
> ATTORNEY SINCLAIR: Dr. Devlin, were you present during the original altercation in the squad room between Captain Fraker and Lieutenant Rodriguez?
>
> DR. DEVLIN: No.
>
> ATTORNEY SINCLAIR: So you don't know, when Captain Fraker said, "I hope the bastard's dead," what or who or any of the circumstances that was in regard to.
>
> DR. DEVLIN: No, but I took—
>
> ATTORNEY SINCLAIR: (interrupting) Thank you. (pause) Dr. Devlin— who are you dating?
>
> ADA HAYWOOD: Objection.
>
> ATTORNEY SINCLAIR: Goes to bias.
>
> JUDGE: The witness can answer....

No, things were not going well for our side. But how could this happen? How can Sinclair twist things, make fun of Dr. Devlin, make it seem plausible that dead-drunk Fraker might have outdrawn a sober Rodriguez? Linking Devlin and her lover could make the jury suspect that she is biased—that will cast doubt on even her scientific, medical testimony. Why can he do that in a court of law? How does this all work?

To answer that, we have to look at language. This is actually all about language. Let's step back from courtroom procedure and look at the mechanisms we humans actually use to communicate. Once we have a handle on that, we can examine why the language used in courtroom interactions is so different from that in normal conversation. Then we'll look at the way this plays out in the courtroom on *NYPD Blue* and also how it relates to the show's police interrogations. Along the way, we'll examine the role of language as a prime means of establishing who you are, what group you belong to and which ones you don't.

In Court, We Play by Different Rules

In a famous real-life case, the president of a bankrupt movie production company was asked by a creditor's lawyer about assets. The creditors were trying to find out if any money was stashed in European banks.

QUESTION: Do you have any bank accounts in Swiss banks, Mr. Bronston?

ANSWER: No, sir.

QUESTION: Have you ever?

ANSWER: The company had an account there for about six months, in Zurich. (*Bronston v. United States*, 409 U.S. 354 [1973])[4]

Would you be surprised, after reading Mr. Bronston's answer, to learn that in addition to the company account, he himself *also* had a large *personal* Swiss bank account? In fact, he had had one, and for five years he had written and deposited checks for over $180,000. So—did he "lie" on the stand? A court thought so, and convicted Bronston of perjury,

---

[4] My discussion of *Bronston v. United States* is adapted from *Legal Language* by Peter Tiersma (1999: 178–9), an invaluable book I use as a text in my university forensic linguistics courses. Anyone interested in forensic linguistics, or any aspect of the intersection of language and law should read it. Tiersma also maintains a Web site that constantly updates the information in the book.

the crime of lying under oath. But the Supreme Court of the United States unanimously reversed his conviction. Why?

The Unspoken Rules about Speaking

The prosecution in Bronston's perjury trial said that when he answered the question by only talking about the *company's* bank account, Bronston had falsely implied that he had never had a *personal* Swiss bank account. And of course he had indeed *falsely* implied that—by the normal rules of language, anyway. There is, in language, what linguists and philosophers call the Cooperative Principle, which sums up what speakers actually expect in conversation: that the other guy will cooperate with us.

Let's say Susan and Joan are college students who live in the same dorm. On Susan's way to a party one night, she passes by Joan's room and sees her reading.

"Aren't you going to the party, Joan?" asks Susan.

Joan shrugs, barely looking up: "I have a test tomorrow." (from "Carol and Lara" in Yule 1996: 145–6)

I've added a bit to Yule's story: Relieved, Susan goes off to eat, then later shows up at the party where—you guessed it—Joan is sitting with Susan's boyfriend as they hold hands and gaze into each other's eyes.

"Joan," Susan says through clenched teeth, "didn't you tell me you weren't coming to the party?"

Joan looks quizzically at Susan, furrowing her brow in concentration. "No, I don't remember ever saying *that*."

You wouldn't be surprised if Joan's last name was Bronston, because she has of course pulled the same trick. Just what was that trick? She pretended to cooperate—she pretended to follow the normal unspoken rules about speaking—but she didn't.

Whose Side Are You On, Anyway?—
The Cooperative Principle

The philosopher H. P. Grice outlined the components of the Cooperative Principle. One component (there are four all together) is the Maxim of Quantity, which says that to cooperate you should give *enough* information, but *no more* information than necessary. This describes the fact that people who run off at the mouth, who repeat the same information ten times in a row, who answer "How are you today?" as if the asker were *actually* asking for information about how they were today, who volunteer information about things no one even obliquely asked about, are not cooperating. People who do not give enough information are also not cooperating, because *the assumption is always that they have cooperated.*

One more example. You want to know how many children Mrs. Smith has, so you ask. She responds, "Hmm, well, let's see, there's Jenny who's eight, and Johnny who's six. Yep." Assuming that she has cooperated, you infer that the woman has two children. Later you find out she has seven children. She hasn't "lied." She just hasn't told the truth—or at least, she hasn't cooperated. She does have Jenny and Johnny. That's true. It was *you* who assumed from what she said that she *only* had those two. But that isn't what she literally said. And Joan, if she lives long enough, might say to Susan, "But—I *do* have a test." We assume people have given us *enough* information to figure out the larger meaning. And people usually do, or other people stop talking to them.

Why does language work this way? Isn't it sloppy? Doesn't it leave so much of the meaning liable to fall between the cracks? The answer is that it isn't sloppy, it's efficient. Joan doesn't have to explain that *because* she has a test tomorrow, she can't go to the party, because if she did maybe she would get back too late to do enough studying, etc., etc. She can just say, "I have a test tomorrow," and Susan will figure out all the rest—IF they are both cooperating. But as soon as one person realizes the other isn't cooperating, the rules change—next time, you can be sure that Susan will ask some follow-up questions to be sure she has the *whole truth* (and nothing but the truth) about her friend's plans.

That's the situation—*not cooperating*—we have in the courtroom. And everyone is aware of it, or should be. And everyone has to take precautions. If they don't, then the fault is their own. That's why the Supreme Court reversed Bronston's perjury conviction. It pointed out that Bronston's answer was literally true, even if it contained what linguists call an *invited inference*. (Joan's invited inference was that she wasn't going to the party, and Mrs. Smith invited the inference that she had only two children.) It is the responsibility of the questioning lawyer to be sure that an answer is not only the truth, but the whole truth. But as we see, even lawyers can't always drop their lifetime of training in using the Cooperative Principle.

This Program Has Been Prerecorded: Schemas

Expectations about the way the world works structure our understanding of language in another way as well. People act as if they had prerecorded scripts stored in their heads, and when some bit of language reminds them of one, the script starts to roll and fills in all sorts of blanks.

Look at Susan and Joan again. Remember we pointed out that Joan can just say, "I have a test tomorrow," and Susan will figure out all the rest. The Maxim of Quantity means she shouldn't go on and on about something that Susan can easily figure out for herself from the short trigger ("I have a test tomorrow") that Joan gave her. Why can she figure out the rest? Because Susan has stored in her mind somewhere a script, a storyline that includes "A college student has a test tomorrow, and she can't go to a party, because if she did go she might not have time to study. If you don't study enough you might fail, and students don't like to fail. Students are people who go to school. School is...." That is why Joan can just say, "I have a test..." and all the information gets filled in. This is how we communicate (efficient, isn't it?) and remember things: by utilizing these knowledge frameworks, which psychologists call *schemas*. Psychologists define them as

> mental representation[s] of some aspect of experience, based on prior experience and memory, structured in such a way as to facilitate (and sometimes to distort) perception, cognition, the drawing of inferences or the interpretation of new information in terms of existing knowledge. (Colman 2001: 653)

The linguist Deborah Tannen, describing how schemas function in language, notes the ramifications of prior experiences being stored in an organized way: *expectations*.

> The prior experience of organized knowledge then takes the form of expectations about the world, and in the vast majority of cases, the world, being a systematic place, confirms these expectations, saving the individual the trouble of figuring things out anew all the time. (Tannen 1993: 20–21)

This is the design of human language. Quick, efficient—and heavily reliant on humans' excellent problem-solving ability. It's like a new puzzle each time someone speaks. You have to put two and two together and figure out which schema the speaker had in her mind.

The trouble is, there is an infinity of possible schemas. Based on who the speaker is, where she is right now, what she does for a living and where she grew up—how, one might ask, could her schema be the same as mine? It's pretty obvious that schemas vary greatly by culture and country, and a lot can go wrong if schemas don't match. But usually, the understanding that results is, if not perfect, at least sufficient. Sometimes, however, the result is an understanding that is less than sufficient—in fact, not at all what the speaker intended. One of my favorite examples is a story where different schemas are triggered through purposeful manipulation (from Sanford and Garrod 1981 [quoted in Yule 1996: 146–7]):

John was on his way to school last Friday. He was really worried about the math lesson.

Okay, now who is John? Most people would say he is a schoolboy. How is he going to school? Is he swimming? Skydiving? Nobody says that. Why? Although notice that the story doesn't specify how he is going, most people infer that he is on a bus, or walking—modes of transportation that would fit with the "schoolboy" schema. Next line:

Last week he had been unable to control the class.

Now the inference is that John is a teacher. Now we visualize him on the way to school in a car. Next:

It was unfair of the math teacher to leave him in charge.

Now he's back to being a student. Last:

After all, it is not a normal part of a janitor's duties.

A humorous demonstration of triggering different schemas in real life is the accidental double-meaning headlines that the *Columbia Journalism Review* collects. These allow for the conjuring up of some pretty wild schemas: Club Hears Trees Talk at Meeting; Dr. Ruth Talks about Sex with Newspaper Editors; Police Nab Students with Pair of Pliers; Grilled Duck Shows off Skill. Ask yourself: why are there different interpretations? How do we know which is the "real" interpretation? We test all the different possible schemas in the blink of an eye and see which might make more sense within the larger schemas of everyday possibilities. (A duck, once grilled, is unlikely to show off any skill other than the cook's.)

Another good example of a schema or a script is the story I made up about Joan and Susan. Reread it and see just how little detail I actually included. I could get away with giving so little information because most of us have already stored in our head a very lighthearted script of "conniving friend steals dumb boyfriend."

The Courtroom

Now we're ready to go back to the courtroom scene from *NYPD Blue*. Remember, Captain Fraker of the IAB had shot Lieutenant Rodriguez in his office and was in turn shot by Detective Ortiz. Fraker was being tried for attempted murder. His story was that Rodriguez drew his gun first. This is the scene in its entirety:

ASSISTANT DISTRICT ATTORNEY VALERIE HAYWOOD: And did you have occasion to treat Captain Fraker that afternoon?

DR. DEVLIN: Yes. He was brought into the ER with a gunshot wound to his spine at about 6:15. I stabilized him and he was sent to Neurosurgery.

ADA HAYWOOD: Did you draw his blood?

DR. DEVLIN: I did. Per procedure the sample was sent to our lab for analysis.

ADA HAYWOOD: And what were the results of that analysis?

DR. DEVLIN: Mr. Fraker's blood alcohol content registered point two-five.

ADA HAYWOOD: And in your expert medical opinion, would that BAC be sufficient to impair the motor skills of a man of the defendant's height and weight?

DR. DEVLIN: Absolutely.

ADA HAYWOOD: So the speed at which one could, for example, reach for a gun—would that be impacted?

DR. DEVLIN: Hand-eye coordination would be substantially diminished.

ADA HAYWOOD: So in your opinion, if a man as intoxicated as Captain Fraker saw a sober man draw his own gun, would Captain Fraker be able to outdraw the sober man?

DEFENSE ATTORNEY JAMES SINCLAIR: Objection, speculation—this is a medical witness, not a cowgirl. (jurors laugh, smile at each other)

JUDGE: Sustained.

ADA HAYWOOD: Dr. Devlin, during the course of your treatment of the defendant did he say anything to you?

DR. DEVLIN: He said, "I hope the bastard's dead." He kept repeating that.

ADA HAYWOOD: Thank you.

ATTORNEY SINCLAIR: Dr. Devlin, were you present during the original altercation in the squad room between Captain Fraker and Lieutenant Rodriguez?

DR. DEVLIN: No.

ATTORNEY SINCLAIR: So you don't know, when Captain Fraker said, "I hope the bastard's dead," what or who or any of the circumstances that was in regard to.

DR. DEVLIN: No, but I took—

ATTORNEY SINCLAIR: (interrupting) Thank you. (pause) Dr. Devlin— who are you dating?

ADA HAYWOOD: Objection.

ATTORNEY SINCLAIR: Goes to bias.

JUDGE: The witness can answer.

DR. DEVLIN: (in a small voice) John Clark.

ATTORNEY Sinclair: I'm sorry?

DR. DEVLIN: (moves her mouth closer to microphone) John Clark.

ATTORNEY SINCLAIR: A detective in the 15th Precinct—right?

DR. DEVLIN: Yes.

ATTORNEY SINCLAIR: And were you dating Detective Clark during this incident?

DR. DEVLIN: I was.

ATTORNEY SINCLAIR: Nothing further.

ADA HAYWOOD: Redirect, Your Honor. Dr. Devlin, have you discussed your testimony at all with Detective Clark?

DR. DEVLIN: No.

ADA HAYWOOD: And has Detective Clark influenced your testimony in any way?

DR. DEVLIN: No.

ADA HAYWOOD: Thank you, Doctor.

Competing Schemas

How can we characterize this exchange of questions and answers? Perhaps we should call it a *Battle of the Schemas* since each side was trying to trigger schemas in the minds of the jurors. Haywood was trying to have the jurors play in their minds a film clip with the schema or script (or, as a similar concept is called in the law, a "narrative") of "angry vindictive drunk careening around and in frustration pulling his gun to kill the man he hates." This wouldn't be too difficult for any of us to reasonably piece together. Earlier in the show (before this scene) Sinclair suggested a schema in which Rodriguez drew on Fraker first. Here, Haywood tried to show that such a schema was impossible, saying, "If a man as intoxicated as Captain Fraker saw a sober man draw his own gun," Fraker would *not* be able to outdraw the sober man. Notice that her questioning, however, was weak, convoluted and hard to follow. She should have made clear, decisive statements (as her opponent did later) because she knew that Devlin, her own witness, who wanted to help her, would agree. But instead, she was unclear and didn't effectively use what (at least at first) was her very believable star witness. Research has shown that jurors are more likely to believe "authoritative, objective" witnesses—ones like Dr. Devlin, who show their education and training by using technical terms like "per procedure" and "hand-eye coordination would be substantially diminished"—witnesses who are considered to have an "expert medical opinion" and are sure of themselves on the stand.

In any event, defense attorney Sinclair threw a monkey wrench into all this. He sabotaged Haywood and Devlin's schemas, established his own and broke down the "authoritative, objective" status of Devlin.

The very first thing Sinclair said, about Devlin being "a medical witness, not a cowgirl," was calculated both to a) block ADA Haywood's script about Fraker being too drunk to outdraw Rodriguez by claiming even a medical witness could not make that conclusion, and b) break down Dr. Devlin's status by comparing her to the somewhat unserious figure of a "cowgirl," suggesting to the jurors that Devlin (who is young and quite beautiful) shared qualities with a cowgirl: a young woman, valued for physical talents rather than intellectual abilities.

This image further invited the jurors to attach to Devlin any other less-than-authoritative, or even downright sexual, thoughts about cowgirls they might have had floating around in their heads. Also, importantly, Sinclair created a bond with the jurors by making them laugh. Research shows that the more the jurors like a lawyer, the more believable they will find his or her side, perhaps because the *lawyer* is more believable (that is, they are more likely to assume he or she is being cooperative).

Sinclair tried to derail the "vindictive killer" storyline. He refused to allow the inference clearly invited by Devlin's testimony—that when

Fraker repeated the phrase, "I hope the bastard's dead," he meant Rodriguez. Don't we have to assume that Fraker is referring to *somebody* when he says that? The most logical inference would be the somebody that he had just *shot*! But Sinclair blocked this: no inferences please, just the facts, ma'am. Note Sinclair didn't ask Dr. Devlin what schema she believed since he knew Devlin inferred Fraker meant Rodriguez. Instead, Sinclair asked questions to which he knew the answer must be "no" ("no" has such a nice sound in the mouth of a witness you don't want the jury to believe), and invited the jury to make the inference that since Devlin wasn't *at* the shooting, she couldn't know who Fraker was talking about. This is very illogical—she could know who Fraker shot without having to witness it herself—but it worked, because it threw Devlin off her stride and confused her briefly, allowing Sinclair to create the impression that she was making *unwarranted* inferences. Sinclair was building a schema in the minds of the jurors about Devlin as witness: *here is a witness who draws conclusions that she shouldn't; therefore nothing she says should be believed.* In so doing he dragged their minds away from the most obvious inference, that it was Rodriguez whom Fraker hoped was dead. (Good thing this all happened quicker than it takes to explain it. Of course, that's why schema-building makes language use so efficient and economical.)

Then with an impassive face Sinclair went in for the kill. While Devlin was still off balance from his interruption of her answer about Fraker, he hit her with the question, "Who are you dating?" She answered weakly, although audibly. Sinclair asked again, both to draw more attention to the answer and to imply that she had wanted to avoid answering in the first place. He established she was dating a detective from the squad, and was dating him at the time of the shooting, and asked no more questions. He left it to the jurors to build their own schema. And a strong one it was, as we saw how ineffectual Haywood was in trying to dismantle it. Haywood asked, in essence, if sleeping with someone could cause a bias in your testimony. "Oh, no," said Devlin. But the denials did nothing to rattle the well-known script of lying to help someone you love.

The language of the courtroom is unlike any other in its manipulation and blocking of schemas. And "conversation" there is unique in another important aspect as well: lawyers have all the power. They have the absolute ability to ask questions, which, if not disallowed by the judge, the witness *must* answer. The judge said, when Sinclair asked who Devlin was dating, "The witness can answer." He meant, of course, she had no other choice but to answer.

Further, a witness must answer *only* the question put to her. As we saw above, Sinclair observed that since she wasn't in the squad room during the shooting, she didn't know "when Captain Fraker said, 'I hope the bastard's dead,' what or who or any of the circumstances that was in regard to." This was as leading a question as there can be. There was only one answer possible, and after she gave it, the rules of the courtroom gave Sinclair every right to cut her off. *This isn't a conversation.* This isn't speakers having a give-and-take. This is a closely regulated process of extracting information from witnesses through question and answer.

The Law Is Language

Language is at the very center of the American legal system. We need, of course, Dr. Devlin's medical science to interpret blood chemistry. And the police lab uses physics to reconstruct the trajectory of a bullet. But we need *linguistics*, the science that analyzes language, just as much, to understand and interpret how language works. We saw how even hard scientific evidence, something most of us feel it is impossible to fake or change, must itself be presented—and therefore interpreted—through language.

Further, most of what *happens* in the law is not "hard evidence." What happens in the law is *language* (see Leonard 2003). We write laws through language, issue subpoenas and warrants, give testimony and write contracts. Attorneys use language to write briefs, make opening and closing arguments, question and cross-examine witnesses. Judges issue orders, write decisions, and charge juries. The police canvass for information, question, interview and interrogate, and suspects provide alibis and explanations, claim, deny and confess—all through language.

We have seen how changeable and slippery language is, how open to interpretation it can be—how in the right hands, or mouth, it can paint pictures in people's minds and block others from presenting their side of an argument. A letter sent to *Atlantic Monthly* to complain about this state of affairs (in response to a November 2000 article) demanded language that had "clarity":

> Nuance is highly overrated. In business and law the LAST thing I want is nuance. In nuance is a legal case. I want stark, bleak, naked, cold and heartless clarity in my business documents. And that is what I shall have.

> Fat chance.

INTERROGATIONS: POLICE INTELLIGENCE-GATHERING VS. DRAMATIC DEVICE

Interrogations as Core Dramatic Device

NYPD Blue is a great TV show. It isn't, of course, reality. On a TV show (even so-called "reality" shows), everything that happens or doesn't happen must be for *dramatic* reasons, not because it is a slice of real life. For example, on *NYPD Blue* we never see the police record anything with video, or voice tape, or use a stenographer, or even scribble notes when they interrogate a murder suspect. How often have you ever seen anyone on the show read *Miranda* rights? "You have the right to remain silent …," a mainstay even of other cop shows, usually isn't bothered with. When the detectives haul in a perp (someone suspected of having perpetrated, or committed, a crime), they do not routinely interrogate that perp with his or her lawyer present, since it wouldn't advance the ball dramatically as well as the kind of police interrogations we do see on the show.

On *NYPD Blue* interrogation scenes serve a key dramatic function: they let the detectives mingle with perps and witnesses and family members. They allow the plot to unfold, as piece after piece of new information, detail after detail of interaction, all combine to build the jigsaw puzzle of each player's personality and character. The interrogations are a great vehicle for establishing who everyone is and what they are made of. And this is largely done not through actions—think how rare action shots really are on *NYPD Blue*—but through language.

Before we look at *NYPD Blue*'s more drama-oriented interrogations, let's step back (as we did before with courtroom procedures) and look at some underlying scientific principles of getting information from interrogations.

The Goals of Real-World Interrogation

The sociolinguist Roger Shuy[5] says that we might want to evaluate the information that comes from police interrogations by the standards of police *intelligence analysis*, and until we are sure of the subject's guilt, at least allow for the possibility that the perp *didn't* do it:

---

[5] Roger Shuy virtually founded forensic linguistics as a field in the U.S. He has written many excellent and readable books on the subject. A superb book I use as a text, immensely popular with my students, is *The Language of Confession, Interrogation and Deception* (Sage Publications, 1998).

Unless the evidence is explicit and noncontroversial, intelligence analysts, by definition, pose multiple hypotheses about the information they receive. One hypothesis, of course, is that the suspect is guilty. But efficient intelligence analysts cannot stop here. They must also pose hypotheses of innocence: how can the data be interpreted to support the suspect's claim of innocence? ... In fact, the role of the intelligence analyst is to probe allegations and suggestions of criminal activity, rather than to build an evidential case. (Shuy 1998: 16)

Intelligence analysis—looking at information from different angles to see how the evidence could support the suspect's innocence as well as guilt, and imagining multiple other explanations for the data at hand— is superior in many ways to just trying to pin the crime on an available suspect. First, to assume innocence is more just. Second, we will be more efficient at getting criminals off the street because we are trying to find the person who *actually* did the crime, not merely someone to charge with it. Third, we avoid wasting sums of money prosecuting people who turn out to be not only innocent but not convictable. Shuy gives the famous example of the *United States v. John DeLorean*, a case with which he was involved.[6] Here the prosecution and the police never entertained the possibility that DeLorean was innocent until they lost the case and he was acquitted.

The secret police in Mombasa, Kenya, once questioned me when I lived in East Africa, years ago during the reign of Jomo Kenyatta. Special Branch accused me of operating as a spy, gathering intelligence along the politically sensitive North Coast near the border with Somalia, and trolling for information in the bars and clubs of Mombasa, Africa's second-largest port. The most prominent, *prima facie* evidence against me, I believe, was that I was an American who fluently spoke three dialects of Swahili. The most obvious schema that explained that odd state of affairs was that I was a spy. They brought me into a room. No one asked me a thing; I was told what I had been doing and that I was guilty.

But I wasn't a spy, and quite luckily for me I could prove it. I possessed (and providentially had on me) a document issued by the Office of the President of Kenya that declared I had research clearance and was a researcher from Columbia University. The document showed that the very activities I was accused of doing were what I was actually supposed

---

[6] See Shuy's 1993 *Language Crimes*

to be doing: sailing around the North Coast on Swahili dhows and making occasional visits to big-city Mombasa where I could get my recording equipment fixed. I was on a Fulbright Fellowship to do research on the Swahili dialects of the North Coast.

Interrogations Versus Interviews

Situations like these, and many others in which one is questioned, highlight a distinction Shuy draws between interviews and interrogations: In *interrogations* it is very clear who is in charge—who has the power. In *interviews* the power relationship at least seems more equal. It is in *interviews*, Shuy notes, that the police often get the better intelligence. There are many reasons for this, some obvious and some that will probably surprise. We'll come back to this later.

Obviously if you are being beaten, or if you fear for your safety or your life, you will likely confess to anything you're told to.[7] Even if you are only badgered, or threatened, or lied to, you will still say things in response to those stimuli, and not necessarily because they are the truth. This makes the questioners very efficient—if they don't particularly care about the truth and only want you to confess.

How to Get the Best Information: Don't Ask Questions

Of course, we can assume most police are interested in catching the person who actually did a crime, not merely finding someone to pin it on while letting the guilty person go on to other ones. So we need a method of finding out who did do the crime before trying to get a confession. It is almost universally agreed—by police interrogation experts, by psychologists and by linguists—that there is a certain maximally efficient way of getting information:

> Interrogation manuals uniformly suggest that questioning is most effective if the suspect is first asked an open-ended question that enables him or her to tell his or her story uninterrupted. At that point, the officer can follow up with *wh-* questions for the specifics of who, what, where and when. Then, probes follow, usually with questions that can be answered with either a yes or a no. The

---

[7] Although I might be tempted to say that I could have withstood anything the secret police inquisitors threw at me, the truth is that right from the beginning of my interrogation in Kenya I would have readily confessed to having assassinated President Lincoln.

principle here is that the best evidence is that which is self-gener-
ated and not influenced by the question or the questioner. (Shuy
1998: 147–8)

This last point is crucial: *subjects generate the best evidence all by themselves, not in response to questions*. Later I'll discuss an interview style that
maximizes the information a subject will produce. Meanwhile, consider
a stunning reason to let witnesses talk before asking *any* questions.

Questions Can Actually Change a Witness's View of "Reality"

It comes as a great surprise to most people that questioners can *change*
someone's memory just by the way they conduct their questioning. People have the unfounded notion, learned from our culture, that one's
senses "record" reality the same way film records an image. In this view,
memory retrieves the reality-record from some mental file and produces
it for the consciousness to examine. Actual data, however, seem to support quite a different view—that memory reinvents reality each time it
is called upon. A better analogy, actually, than photo film is a dream.
Disjointed half-images float around our heads and we hammer together
a meaning out of them. But there is no "reality" in a dream to record
in the first place; nor is there, it would seem, in the world outside of
dreams, either. We cobble together some meaning from what our senses
tell us is happening in the real world, but we only perceive what we are
led to believe we will perceive. The real world does not actually exist.
Or if it does exist, we don't have access to it. What we do have access
to are schemas. And as we will see, sometimes questioners accidentally
change a witness's memory by calling up certain schemas—and sometimes they do it on purpose.

Lawyers and others develop skills in language that change people's
perception of reality. As we look at these techniques, they may at first
seem like sleight of hand. But they are quite simple and use established
scientific linguistic principles—like the schema-building we discussed
in the last section—to alter the memories of even eyewitnesses. Study
after study shows the effects. For example, asking questions with in-
serted "presuppositions"—assumptions built in to the very structure
of the language used—caused subjects to remember a barn in a film of
an accident they had seen a week before—though there was no barn in
the film:

[S]ubjects saw a film of an accident and were asked the key question "How fast was the white sports car going when it passed the barn while traveling along the country road?" No barn actually existed. One week later, these subjects returned and answered a new set of questions, including "Did you see a barn?" Compared to a control group whose initial questionnaire had not mentioned a barn, these "barn" subjects were much more likely to report that they had seen the nonexistent barn. (Loftus: 3–14)

What these researchers discovered won't surprise us too much if we remember our examples of the Cooperative Principle and its interaction with schema-building. As we saw with Bronston, and Susan and Joan, and the Battle of the Schemas with Haywood and Sinclair, we automatically assume that people are cooperating with us as we try to make sense of things and construct or pull up schemas. A barn fits quite nicely into the standard schema of a country road. If we had been watching that film, we would no doubt be focusing on the car, so we might not have noticed if there was a barn. When someone asks about a barn it suggests to us a higher probability of there having been a barn than if no one mentioned a barn at all: we think, "Now that you ask, it would make sense that maybe there was a barn."

In another study, choosing loaded words to ask about accidents in a movie caused people to remember the speed of filmed cars differently. The question issued was: "About how fast were the cars going when they hit/smashed into each other?" Those asked with *hit* estimated an average of 34.0 mph; those with *smashed* averaged 40.8 mph. Further, when asked a week later, "Did you see any broken glass?" those originally asked with *smashed* were more likely to answer yes than those originally asked with *hit*. There was no broken glass in the film (Loftus 10).

So, subtle and almost imperceptible differences in the wording of questions can influence witnesses' recall of events. We can change "reality" by asking questions in a certain way. A superb example of this is from Richard C. Wydick (*The Ethics of Witness Coaching*, 17 Cardozo L. Rev. 1 [1995], discussed in Tiersma 1999: 173). A lawyer interviews a witness before going into court:

Q: When Bloggs came into the pub, did he have a knife in his hand?
A: I don't remember.
Q: Did you see him clearly?
A: Yes.

Q: Do people in that neighborhood often walk into pubs with knives in their hands?
A: No, certainly not.
Q: If you had seen Bloggs with a knife in his hand, would you remember that?
A: Yes, of course.
Q: And you don't remember any knife.
A: No, I don't remember any knife.

What started out as "I don't remember" may come out at trial as follows:

Q: When Bloggs came into the pub, did he have a knife in his hand?
A: No, he did not. (Tiersma: 173)

In open court, the first exchange might very well have been objected to. But in a lawyer's office, there is no such scrutiny. The question "If you had seen Bloggs with a knife in his hand, would you remember that?" should remind us of the barn example, but in reverse. It was easy to suggest a barn, since a normal schema of a country road includes a barn. If your most normal schema is that people in a particular neighborhood NEVER walk into pubs with knives in their hands, it might take a lot for you to notice if someone actually did, because you wouldn't be looking for it and it might be easy to overlook if it weren't made obvious—especially in a place like a bar, where there are probably many things going on to distract your attention. So the fact that you didn't see something out of place in a very familiar context doesn't mean it wasn't there. There is a well-known experiment that demonstrates how an unexpected event—even an absurd, jarring event like a person in a gorilla suit walking blithely through a basketball game—will not be noticed by a large percentage of the audience because they are given a task like counting passes that keeps their consciousness on the game itself. "Observers often do not see unanticipated objects and events," say the researchers. (Simons and Chabris 1999: 1065) They only "see" what makes sense in the context of the game.

So Don't Ask Questions
if You Want What Really Happened

Police departments know these principles. During the infamous Washington, D.C., sniper attacks in 2003, the police repeatedly broadcast the following advice for anyone actually witnessing something: call the police and do NOT speak to anyone. The authorities had been confused and misled several times by witnesses imagining details that had not existed, and they wanted witnesses to have as unrestructured a memory as was possible.

The process of triggering schemas can work against you if you are trying to find out what really happened. Thus if you *don't want* to shape people's memory of events, say many experts, *don't ask* them questions.

There is a professional technique called SCAN, invented by A. Sapir, which is based on this. Shuy states that the very heart of Sapir's claim is that "the interviewer is the most serious obstacle to obtaining information" (1998: 105). SCAN technique asks people who have some knowledge of the incident under investigation to write a statement on their own, before ever being interviewed. (The statements are then analyzed to see who should be followed up on.)

The Interactional Interview
and the Effective Interrogation

I suggest that the best path to gather intelligence, and to obtain confessions, is a sequence that I call the *Interactional Interview*, based largely on the brilliant *Linguistic Interview* techniques developed by William Labov, one of the world's most respected sociolinguists and experts on interviews. Linguists have analyzed thousands of actual interviews and conversations, and from them distilled techniques and systems that produce the most interaction. My Interactional Interview uses the interview techniques of linguists, modified for forensic purposes.

The Linguistic Interview is designed to start subjects talking, in whatever language, and keep them talking. Linguists are interested in language, in the talk itself, so a linguist normally doesn't use these techniques to get information but rather to get the talk the information is wrapped up in. It's like buying a thousand boxes of cornflakes to get the boxes. Of course, you also wind up with an awful lot of cornflakes.

The Interactional Interview uses the cornflakes, too. The Interactional Interview gathers information from the subject that may, for example, contradict earlier information, or implicate an accomplice, or demonstrate that the subject should not be considered a suspect.

The first step in the Interactional Interview sequence asks the subject to give as unstructured an account as possible, to avoid triggering schemas and to avoid letting the subject know how much the interviewer knows.

Secondly, one asks questions according to techniques that *mimic the dynamic structure of true conversations*. Shuy gives detailed descriptions of effective police interrogations. These reveal a surprising feature: politeness. The questioner takes the point of view of the subject, and lets the subject have an unlimited turn.

Actually, more than an unlimited turn. Shuy describes a technique he has taught students for years and which Labov also taught, which is also used by skilled police interrogators: you simply don't take your turn in the conversation.

You look interested and show clearly that you follow what the subject says. You nod, make feedback responses such as "uh-huh" or "ah" or "umm." But you don't take your turn in the conversation. After a few seconds, the person speaking will start up again (try this at home!), often recycling and elaborating part of the story he or she has just told, and will go on from there without being aware of what has happened. The Linguistic Interview encompasses many other elements that I won't go into here except to note that they all demonstrate a respect for what the subject will say.

I was surprised when I started doing research in forensic linguistics and discovered that skilled police interrogators used techniques that looked very much like the Linguistic Interviews Labov trained me to use for my doctoral research. It is interesting that essentially the same procedures form the core of the best and most effective police interrogations.

If the most effective and valid interrogation is that which mimics genuine conversation, the true power differential between the police and the subject is barely reflected in the conversation. The questioner guides. As much as possible, the subject is allowed to speak freely, without interruption.

The questioning itself should follow well-accepted principles of linguistics and the literature on interrogation procedures:

First: ask open-ended questions

Then: ask *wh-* [who, what, when, etc.] questions

If necessary: probe with yes-no questions

Then: repeat the cycle with another open-ended question (Shuy 1998: 178)

Allow for face-saving; never browbeat. Let subjects show either consistency or inconsistency in their stories. This latter is the proverbial "enough rope to hang oneself with."

Shuy is emphatic that "investigators should begin the questioning of suspects with an information interview and continue to gather facts until such time as the suspect's fact reporting becomes inconsistent. At such a point, it is proper to move into a genuine interrogation in which the goal is to elicit a confession..." (192).

NYPD Blue's Police Intelligence-Gathering

In a typical *NYPD Blue* show, we open with a crime scene, usually of a murder. The detectives arrive, are briefed by the uniformed cops as to what is so far known, and examine the crime scene and the DOA. (DOA actually stands for Dead On Arrival to a hospital, but is also used to refer to any dead person.) Witnesses—for example, the superintendent of the apartment building, or the plumber who found the body, or perhaps the deceased's roommate—are waiting to be interviewed. Often one team of detectives announces they are going to canvass, which essentially means to go through the area and see if they can find anyone who has any knowledge to share, while another team examines the body and talks to the assembled witnesses. The questioning of witnesses is done pretty much as the experts would suggest: begin with open-ended questions and proceed through to more detailed ones, letting the witnesses self-generate the information. Often we then see the detectives back in the squad room, discussing leads and theories and processing the phone "dumps" (records of calls) and deciding what to do next. Later in the show we likely see them walking up the stationhouse stairs with someone they want to question, either as a witness or a suspect. It is clear from the dialogue that no questioning has been done before they sit down at the table in one of the interrogation rooms. As noted before, no recordings or notes ever seem to be made, and no one seems to be *Miranda*-warned of his or her right to avoid self-incrimination. Typically the show's detectives "have a go" at the perp and seem to hope that by accusing or badgering him he will confess. If that doesn't work, they might lie to the perp and claim that they have information that contradicts the perp's alibi, or say that they have witnesses or hard evidence that clearly incriminates him. Witnesses and suspects are also questioned at their homes or places of business. Wherever they are questioned, the detectives make a very big deal of avoiding letting suspects request that their lawyers be present. When a suspect seems like he or she is about to "lawyer up"—refuse to talk except through a lawyer—the detectives get agitated and often attempt to forestall him or her. They suggest to the suspect that anyone who wants to have a lawyer present is not co-operating—and probably has something to hide, because otherwise he wouldn't need a lawyer: "When you start saying things like you want a lawyer that puts up a red flag with us, Mr. Smith."

But even though interrogations on *NYPD Blue* are chiefly dramatic devices, the most effective interrogations often follow the very interview techniques that have been shown to work so well in real life.

Take Det. Bobby Simone's series of interactions with a man who raped and killed his own little son. Simone is a master interrogator, probably the most skillful of all the characters to appear on the show. One of the most effective stories was the two-part episode "Lost Israel," about a rape-murder of a little boy in Tompkins Square Park, an area in the Lower East Side rife with derelicts and shooting galleries. The detectives gradually realized that though it had seemed that a homeless man was guilty, the killer was actually the boy's own father, Steve Egan. Sipowicz wanted to "tune up" Egan, to beat the truth out of him, but Simone's cooler and more calculating head prevailed. Simone just talked to the father, and as much as he despised him, he maintained a conversational style. He maintained *politeness*. He let Egan talk.

Eventually, he got the information he needed to be sure Egan was the murderer, but so well had Egan framed the homeless man, Israel, that Simone needed a confession. This would be especially difficult because the man's lawyer carefully controlled every conversation.

Sipowicz had developed a respect and fondness for the homeless Israel, a mute, derelict, elderly black man—yet against his better judgment he badgered him and accused him anew of raping and murdering a child in a staged effort to draw out Egan, who was watching the interrogation.

As a result, Egan evaded his own lawyer to come and talk to Simone, ostensibly to ask him to tell another detective to leave Egan's wife out of the questioning, but actually because he wanted to talk, one to one, without an intermediary. Simone let Egan talk and talk, only guiding, never badgering or confronting: quite a contrast to a Sipowicz tune-up.

> EGAN: You impress me as an intelligent and reasonably sensitive man.... I told you my plans, my friend, so please get out of my way!

SIMONE: (silence)

EGAN: I'm not prepared to dispute you are my friend, and I could use a friend very much, but at the same time you are a detective whose job is attributing guilt.

SIMONE: That is for lawyers and the courtroom. I am trying to understand what happened here.

EGAN: I thought you were trying to forgive everyone.

SIMONE: You know there is forgiveness. You know there's forgiveness. I need you to help me understand.

EGAN: Well, I'm exhausted. And I'm in a state of hopelessness.

SIMONE: That's all right. That's all right. Steve—you brought me here. I need you to tell me why.

Egan told Simone that God told him to do it, so that he would stop abusing his son. He then requested:

EGAN: Kill me. Please. Please. Shoot me in the head.

SIMONE: (close up of stony-faced Simone) I can't.

EGAN: Help me confess. Hurry, get a pencil and paper.

Thus he confessed to Simone, one step ahead of the lawyer chasing them down to stop the interaction. In this case we see Simone using the rules of natural conversation in an effective way for his interrogation purposes. The less he says, the more opportunity he gives Egan to condemn himself with his own words. And when he does talk, his choice of language is very similar to Egan's educated, almost stilted, formality, as in Simone's "Sir, do you think it would be more appropriate to take your concerns to...."

In the next section we'll take a look at how the words people use put them in a certain social category and establish their identity—with either positive or negative consequences. Simone adapted to Egan's way of talking; later we'll see Simone use deep street talk with a junkie. Sipowicz doesn't demonstrate the same range or fluency as Simone does and, as we'll see in the next scene, when he encounters language that emphasizes the social difference between him and someone else, he simply becomes incensed. In contrast Simone is flexible enough to use different ways of talking as another interrogation tool.

You Are What You Speak: Language Is Identity

On one show, Sipowicz and Clark visited a rich big-shot artist, a woman whose former assistant had just been killed. The artist had recently published a photo essay of death row inmates in the *New York Times Magazine* and therefore seemed to the detectives as someone who might not be on the same side as the police. A staple of *NYPD Blue* is confrontation between good-guy working-class detectives and a snobbish effete upper-class poseur, as shown well in the language used in this questioning:

> SIPOWICZ: Detectives Sipowicz and Clark, Miss Howe. Need to ask you some questions about Maureen Dickerson.
>
> HOWE: Regarding what?
>
> SIPOWICZ: Maureen got assaulted in her building. She didn't see who did it.
>
> HOWE: And she accused me? Is she joking?
>
> CLARK: Sounds like you didn't get along well.
>
> HOWE: I never touched her. I may have raised my voice. That's not illegal, is it?
>
> CLARK: You recently raised your voice? Like, when you fired her?
>
> HOWE: I suppose.
>
> CLARK: Tell us about it.
>
> HOWE: She broke a rule about cell phone calls.
>
> SIPOWICZ: And you fired her for breaking it?
>
> HOWE: I fired her because when I was explaining the rules she threw her phone against the wall and called me names.
>
> CLARK: Did the argument end there?
>
> HOWE: It ended when I caught her stealing a Hasselblad case she said was hers for severance.
>
> CLARK: You find anything else missing?
>
> HOWE: No.
>
> SIPOWICZ: You didn't get any feelings of revenge after finding her ripping you off.
>
> HOWE: No!
>
> SIPOWICZ: Friend of mine said you shoot pictures of convicts.
>
> HOWE: That's right.
>
> SIPOWICZ: Any of them owe you favors?
>
> HOWE: I don't understand.
>
> CLARK: A favor—like, "My assistant's a *thief*, I need her ass *kicked*."

SIPOWICZ: Because you don't look like somebody who gets her hands dirty, personally.

HOWE: I don't think I have anything else to say to you.

SIPOWICZ: If you did pull a contract you want to tell us now 'cause it didn't go according to plan. The girl's dead.

HOWE: Maureen's dead.

CLARK: Shot twice.

HOWE: Wow.

SIPOWICZ: Yeah, Lady, "wow." And when we pull your phone records and find contact with a con who rolls over on you because he knows the system better 'n you that's gonna be a huge "wow" because you'll be looking at felony murder.

HOWE: I've had enough. I need to talk to my attorney.

CLARK: That's putting up a red flag to us, calling your attorney.

HOWE: I didn't do anything to Maureen. And I have no more time for this. So you'll just have to deal with my lawyer. (the detectives fall silent)

When the next scene opened back at the police stationhouse, it is reported to the lieutenant that "[Sipowicz and Clark] said the lady lawyered up and she's worth a further look."

Notice in the dialogue how Sipowicz manipulates the "wow" to contrast himself—a serious, down-to-earth cop—against someone who to his mind is a superficial, phony 1960s-leftover liberal (and who, by the way, didn't do it). Where Simone uses such differences strategically, Sipowicz does not. He spits "wow" back to the woman in indignation. And look at the results it gets: the woman lawyers up and refuses to talk.

The cops, of course, also have their own way of talking that marks them as cops. They are no less identifiable by the words they choose than the woman is by hers. So talk can mark you as an outsider—but at the same time serve as an ID card for insiders. It can also prevent outsiders from understanding your speech. Many of the slang and jargon words the cops use on *NYPD Blue* have been noted already—*perp*, *lawyer up, the house, phone dump, DOA, Rat Squad* and *tune up*—and many haven't, *jackpot* (be in trouble), *reach out* (contact someone, usually someone you have known before, often for the purpose of asking a favor), *CI* (confidential informant—that is, a street informant), *a collar* (an arrest—as in *make a collar* and *you're a collar*), *in the wind* (fled, in hiding), *a dump job* (a victim killed one place and left in another), *a floater* (dead body that, after a period of time in water, has risen to the surface), a *mutt* (a lowlife, loser), a *skel* (junkie, lowlife; from *skeleton*—as one real-life NYPD officer explained to my team, "skeletons, what most drug users wind up looking like") and *the job* (the police department—as in *the job wants you to do it this way, contact the job in Baltimore to grab up our fugitive* and *you on the job?*, meaning "are you a cop?").

When it first hit the airwaves, part of the show's appeal was that it used *rough* language, much rougher than that of any other broadcast show of the time. The dramatic justification was obvious. Being a detective in New York is rough business; rough language lent credibility and presence. The other envelope that the show pushed was the "partial nudity" that the network seemed to love "warning" viewers was coming up. The dramatic necessity of seminude simulated sex scenes was not so easily explained, except perhaps by prurient appeal. But the language certainly made sense, for it helped identify tough cops in a famously tough city.

And the producers and writers knew their audience: the rest of the U.S. holds strong stereotypes (otherwise known as *schemas*, right?) about how tough New York is. My own research on attitudes towards New York and New York speech shows this clearly. My favorite example is a woman from Georgia who characterized New York to one of my students as "a place where when you get mugged, nobody notices." Notice that's not "if" you get mugged.

On a visit to the University of California at Los Angeles I was talking to another New Yorker who taught there. We finally noticed a student of his standing in the doorway listening, her eyes wide. She asked me, "Are *you* from New York, too?" I nodded. "Gee," she said, "you guys must be *tough*." On a Disney World bus, an innocent-looking suburban New York college student sat next to a mother and child; they chatted with him and, hearing his accent, asked where he was from. When he answered they got up and moved to the other side of the bus. New York is immoral, impolite, fast-paced, vulgar, angry, bawdy, loud, violent, gritty and, wait, did I forget? *Tough.*

NYPD Blue revels in the fact that it depicts the *New York* Police Department. It pulls out all the stops on schemas viewers have of New York as a place where Anything Can Happen. Moreover, it is set in the Lower East Side, where millions of poor immigrants have lived, a prototypical New York area, a gritty and tough neighborhood. The detectives are the force that keep the world in balance. They toil in the fight between Good and Evil, and they need special powers to fight the special powers of New York Evil. They possess these powers, because they too are New Yorkers. (Even if Sipowicz actually has a Chicago accent.) Who could out-tough Sipowicz and Simone? Who could evade them? Who could con them? Nobody: just listen to them speak.

Street criminals use code words and the grammar and secret language of the street, but they can keep no secrets from tough, street-savvy cops like Simone.

In one episode, Simone and Sipowicz question a drug addict, Larry, whom they "like" (suspect) for the murder of his elderly aunt. Simone uses the street terms *get behind* (act like you believe), *jonesin'* (strongly craving something; here a heroin fix) and *score*, which of course means "to obtain something" (often an illegal substance like drugs). Also *boostin'* (stealing), and *get over* (here, succeed). Larry is black, and when Simone says *aunt* he says it with the Southern and Black pronunciation *ahnt* (with the *a* sound the doctor wants when telling you to say *ah*), and not like most white New Yorkers say it—*ehnt*, same as the insect "ant." He uses what is referred to as "nonstandard *like*" saying, "This is like the worst story I ever heard." This *like*, despised by grammar teachers, is a discourse marker that has various functions in both white and black speech; here it signals a mitigation of claim, giving the impression of camaraderie, as well as extreme informality. Lastly, Simone uses deep New York grammar and asks, "When was the last time you seen [instead of *you saw*] your Aunt Etta?"

> SIMONE: When was the last time you seen your Aunt Etta? ... (Larry gives a smooth but hopelessly farfetched account of where he has been and why he is carrying an envelope with his aunt's jewelry. His leg begins to involuntarily shake: he is starting to withdraw from heroin.) This is like the worst story I ever heard.
>
> LARRY: Yeah, well, that's what happened, man.
>
> SIMONE: Larry, this stuff is so bogus, *you* can't even get behind it. Y'know what I think happened? (Simone pulls in real close to Larry, sticks his face right next to his. Larry starts losing his cool, grimaces.) I think you did something to your aunt that *makes you sick*. (Larry winces.) Now, we could bring this to the DA now as a vicious cold-blooded homicide. (Larry leans away, his breathing labored.) I don't think that was your intention. (pause) Y'see, 'cause I can see you jonesin', so I know that you needed to score. But you didn't sell your aunt's jewelry. We collared you stealing a camera with her jewelry *still in your pocket*. That tells me that you loved her. You say to yourself, "Oh, man, let me just try boostin'

this camera, not sell my aunt's stuff unless I can't get over on the street." (Larry cries.) That what you were thinkin' about?

LARRY: (pleading, crying) Leave me alone, man.

SIMONE: Larry, I been on this job long enough to know where people are at. You don't get right with this, behind jonesin' and getting sicker and sicker, and then all that remorse is gonna start comin' on you and you are definitely gonna be a candidate for some guard at Riker's findin' you hangin' in your cell.

This last part of Simone's lines is especially rife with what linguists call vernacular features. He uses *I been, where people are at* and *behind,* and refers to Riker's Island, the infamous New York City jail.

We've looked at the principles of conversation in the intersection of law and language in courtroom examinations and police interrogations, and the way language establishes who we are. We've seen that in normal conversation people operate according to the Cooperative Principle, but in the courtroom, cooperation in schema-building is not a given. Nor, in many interrogations, are the rules of normal conversations followed— but many skillful interrogators adapt their speech and rules of interaction to mimic natural conversation with very good results. Lastly, we've discussed language's great power to sort people out, to act as a badge of identity. But identity is something you wear, not necessarily something you *are*. Language, in the hands of a skillful user like Detective Simone, can let you change identity to suit your purposes.

References

Cole, P., and Morgan, J. L. (editors). 1975. *Syntax and Semantics: Speech Acts.* Volume 3. New York: Academic.

Colman, Andrew M. 2001. *A Dictionary of Psychology.* 2001. New York: Oxford University Press.

Grice, H. P. 1975. "Logic and Conversation." In Cole, P. and Morgan, J. L. 1975: 41–58.

Leonard, Robert A. 2003. "Linguistics and the Law." *Washington, D.C. Legal Times.*

Loftus, Elizabeth R. *Language and Memories in the Judicial System,* reprinted in Oaks 2001: 3–14

Oaks, Dalin D. (Editor). 2001. *Linguistics at Work: A reader of applications,* Cambridge, MA: Heinle and Heinle.

Sanford, A. J., and Garrod, S. C. 1981. *Understanding Written Language: Explorations of comprehension beyond the sentence.* Chichester, England: John Wiley and Sons.

Shuy, Roger W. 1993. *Language Crimes: The Use and Abuse of Language Evidence in the Courtroom.* Oxford: Blackwell.

Shuy, Roger W. 1998. *The Language of Confession, Interrogation and Deception.* Thousand Oaks, CA: Sage Publications.

Simons, Daniel J., and Chabris, Christopher F. 1999. "Gorillas in Our Midst," *Perception* 28: 1059–1074.

Tannen, Deborah (ed.). 1993. *Framing in Discourse.* New York: Oxford University Press.

Tiersma, Peter. 1999. *Legal Language.* Chicago: University of Chicago Press.

Yule, George. 1985. *The Study of Language.* Cambridge: University Press.

Dr. Robert Leonard is Professor of Linguistics at Hofstra University, and lead researcher at Robert Leonard Associates, a consulting firm. Leonard received his B.A. from Columbia College, where he was elected to Phi Beta Kappa, and his M.A., M.Phil. and Ph.D. from Columbia Graduate School, where he was a Faculty Fellow. He won a Fulbright Fellowship for his overseas Ph.D. research. He may be the only Fulbright Fellow to have performed at Woodstock. While in college he cofounded and led the rock group Sha Na Na and performed at the Woodstock Festival, the Fillmores East and West, on television's Tonight Show, in the Academy Award-winning Woodstock movie and the recently released film Festival Express *with Janis Joplin and the Grateful Dead.*

MAURICE BROADDUS

Sipowicz's Progress: A Slow Walk of Redemption

NYPD Blue portrays something rarely—if ever—seen on network television: a man struggling to define his relationship with God. Unlike overtly religious shows like Touched by an Angel *and* 7th Heaven, NYPD Blue *approaches God, and one man's search for God, with great seriousness and sensitivity.*

FOR ALL THE BROUHAHA about the nudity, sex and profanity that surrounded *NYPD Blue* from the beginning, the meta-narrative of the show—the "drama" as Bill Brochtrup says in the TNT commercials—has been the redemption of Andy Sipowicz. One of the reasons people find it so easy to relate to Andy is that he's one of them: a working stiff who wrestles with alcoholism, racism and homophobia. Andy's struggles aren't sentimentalized: they're real issues that many of us face but don't reveal in polite company.

Andy's relationship with God doesn't get as much play as his battles with alcoholism. What many people forget—often because they get caught up in the legalisms of religion—is that being perfect does not mark one as a truly spiritual individual. It is continual persistence, getting up again and again after stumbling, that leads to holiness.

For a show to truly revolve around the themes of moral and spiritual redemption, the main character must start from a place of loss and sepa-

121

ration. Obviously Andy bottomed out in season one before beginning the arduous process of clawing his way up and turning his life around. Since such a journey begins with loss, the question must be asked: what contributed to Andy's loss of faith?

The rekindling of the relationship between Andy and God is best described as a shotgun wedding, ironically precipitated by Andy's marriage to ADA Sylvia Costas. In season two's "The Bookie and Kooky Cookie" we saw Andy's state of faith (or lack thereof). As part of their wedding preparations, Sylvia wanted the two of them, Andy in particular, to meet her priest. She'd grown up Greek Orthodox and insisted on a Greek Orthodox wedding. Sylvia wanted the priest who had known her since childhood to perform the ceremony and meet her future husband. And most importantly, she wanted her future husband to share in her faith.

His discomfort amusingly palpable and his wariness with strangers (especially priests) quite evident, Andy went into the meeting with his hackles raised. After dancing around each other for a while, Father Kankarides came right out and asked, "Do you believe in God? ... Have you lost your faith?" All Andy could say was "yeah." But that established that he'd believed in God, even if he had lost his way. The Father recognized this and admonished him to not "give up on God; he may not be through with you yet."

That night Andy confessed to Sylvia a story from his early detective days. It was a case involving a missing child, with less-than-helpful parents: the dad was a dog trainer, in town with his German Shepherd, more concerned with attending a special training class; the mom was an alcoholic. The case ended with Andy going at the mom until she confessed that the baby peed while the father was changing him, so the father threw him, fracturing the baby's skull. Andy took the dog, another innocent, and had it killed. He found bits of the baby still in the dog. That was the day he lost his faith.

"I've got faith in you," he then told Sylvia. This was not an empty declaration. Many of the changes to Andy's character did come not so much at Sylvia's insistence; Andy consciously made changes in his life and attitudes because he wanted to be a better man for her. Sylvia was, in many ways, Andy's moral compass.

Many people struggle with the dilemma of finding an acceptable theodicy for the horrors they encounter during the course of a lifetime. The attempts to justify God or explain suffering commonly address the "problem of evil": if God is good and all-powerful, why does evil exist?

Though it seemed like a common stumbling block to belief in God's existence, in the history of philosophical thought this is a fairly recent development.

This problem came about in response to a changing view of God over the last couple hundred years. The image of God as both good and severe once dominated Christian theologies; this was gradually replaced with a belief in a one-dimensional, all-good God. It was difficult to believe that a purely good God could allow horrible things to happen, especially to the innocent. Andy's response to this question of suffering was not unusual—he experienced an acute loss of faith.

Near the end of season three Andy's crisis of non-faith crystallized. In "A Death in the Family" Andy and his partner, Bobby Simone, responded to a robbery-homicide victim who was DOA at the hospital. The victim was Andy's son, Andy, Jr.

Andy had not been much of a father to his son; they hadn't seen each other in years. Andy's absence because of the job, his divorce from Andy, Jr.'s mother and the general quality of his life due to all the alcoholism and womanizing had left them estranged at the beginning of season one. They slowly reconnected over the first three seasons, as Andy made a genuine effort to change. Andy, Jr., was pursuing a career as a cop, following in his father's footsteps. Andy had even been schooling Andy, Jr., on the finer points of police work, allowing the two of them to bond and spend time together.

During the course of the investigation in a "A Death in the Family," we come to find out that Andy, Jr., had been present near a bar during a robbery. He observed a woman about to be sexually assaulted and he stepped in, unlike the other patrons present, and got killed for his trouble. Andy immediately blamed himself, believing that Andy, Jr., was trying to live up to some ideal image that he had created of being a cop ("My concern, did I get this kid killed? I was a big shot. Gave this kid all kinds of lessons.... What did I do?").

Andy tried to keep everything together by sheer force of will—but his grief, anger, regret, concern for his family and the strain of making all of the arrangements proved to be too much for him. Diane Russell—a fellow detective and also a recovering alcoholic—kept assuring him that she was available for walks and AA meetings, but he rebuffed her. Though he'd professed faith in Sylvia, he refused to allow her to comfort him, deciding instead to "take a walk"—a walk that led straight to the local bar. She kicked him out when it became obvious that he couldn't, or wouldn't, pull himself together. Lieutenant Fancy told him to take some days off. Sylvia convinced Andy to meet with her priest, where they had the following exchange:

ANDY: Why should I pay attention to you? Where was God when my boy got killed in that bar?

KANKARIDES: He was there.

ANDY: Then He can kiss my ass. How could He stand there and let that boy die?

KANKARIDES: We're not made to understand God's purposes, Andrew.

ANDY: What, He's trying to punish me? Alright, I deserve punishment. But what about my first wife.... don't you tell me that I did something so bad for Him to do something to them.

KANKARIDES: God is not in the punishment business, Andrew. You are not in the center of the world. Your son's death is not part of some equation. It's a mystery.

At first the viewer is left reeling from the frankness of the exchange. Even in a show trying to be more true with language, the sentiment that God can "kiss my ass" proves to be shocking. Andy's crisis mirrors those found in the Book of Job. After all that Job had been through, his wife gives him the advice to just curse God for his troubles and die for the blasphemy. Religion, spirituality and matters of faith seem to be that last taboo, a topic rarely broached for fear of offending people. *NYPD Blue* broke the mold by portraying a man who was very angry with God.

You can't be angry at someone you don't think exists; few people could work up any real angst over Santa Claus not giving them what they want. It's clear that Andy had a very "Old Testament" view of God. To him God was harsh and only—in the "punishment business"—a God who waits for man to screw up in order to smite him. Andy genuinely communicates his feelings toward God. Andy believed that God bore responsibility for his son's death, so he immediately dispensed with the notion of letting God help him through the dark time.

So what was left? Andy's dignity became the last casualty. Haunted by the ghost of his son, Andy got drunk and tried to break up a group of random punks. When they humiliated him and wrestled his gun from his grasp, Andy stood on the brink of the abyss and ruin. His partner Bobby asked him pointedly: "Do you want people to help you, Andy?"

Andy finally answered, "yes."

His coworkers and loved ones proceeded to haul him back from the edge, into the arms of comfort and redemption. But he hadn't yet turned to God. The end of the story arc found Andy back in conversation with Father Kankarides in "He's Not Guilty, He's My Brother." Andy and Sylvia were preparing for their baby's churching service, in which the infant would receive a blessing and be dedicated to God. Father Kankarides hoped that by accepting the mystery of his son's death, Andy would be unburdened of his pain and loneliness. He encouraged Andy to pray.

At the end of the episode Andy became reacquainted with God. He imitated Sylvia's genuflecting, fumbling as he crossed himself, and took a genuine stab at prayer. He asked God to "take care of my other son, too. Take him to your heart.... Bless and keep my son who's gone and bless and keep all my family. And give me strength to be a good person."

Come season four, Andy faced another critical stop in his spiritual journey. In "Taillight's Last Gleaming," nearly a year after Andy, Jr.'s death, Andy revealed his ongoing grief and God issues. The powerful episode opened with a dream sequence; Andy entered a diner and realized that Andy, Jr., was sitting at the same counter. A bearded trucker sat between them, so Andy asked to switch places with him to be next to his son. Andy, wanting another chance to spend more time with his son, bubbled with unbridled joy, yet he couldn't seem to connect with him.

Andy, Jr., told his father that he "didn't have much time for me when I was alive" and Andy overreacted. Andy, Jr., got up and left, sending his love to Sylvia and Theo. The trucker engaged Andy in small talk, ending with the admonishment "You should have talked through me."

The episode concluded with a change in the setting of the dream. Andy found himself at the bar from "A Death in the Family" where Andy, Jr., was killed. Andy, Jr., and the men who murdered him were present. Andy, Jr., told his father to not interfere, but Andy pummeled them before they could draw their weapons.

But Andy, Jr., still died. Andy once again delivered the haunting line "What did I do?" The bearded trucker appeared again and raised up Andy, Jr.'s body. He heard Andy, Jr.'s disembodied voice say, "That's Jesus Christ, dad. Congratulations on pissing off Jesus." Andy begged the trucker/Jesus for a second chance. "What did you just have?" Jesus asked before reminding Andy to "talk through me."

Andy envisioned Jesus as an average, blue-collar Joe, much like Andy himself. Here's a reversal of God creating man in his image; Andy created God in his image, one that he could relate to. This sequence also provided some closure for Andy by answering his question, "What did I do?" The answer? Nothing. There was nothing Andy could have done to change events, to change what God allowed. By the end of the episode, Andy and God seemed to have come to some sort of tacit understanding.

The last episode of season seven, "The Last Round Up," provided a glimpse of the latest turn in Andy's spiritual walk. Theo was in the hospital for a bone marrow test that would reveal if he had leukemia. Andy had experienced a Job-like run of tragedy, having lost his beloved tropical fish, his son, his wife Sylvia and then his partner. In this episode Andy, a scared and angry father, was faced with the possibility of his little boy dying. Again he found himself coping with events that were wholly out of his control. Rather than crawl back into the bottle, he asked God for help.

Andy found himself in the hospital chapel; he opened his prayer to God by addressing him as "You prick!" Andy asked the questions that most people ask when they're confronted with the possibility of bad things happening to them: "Why is this happening? What have I done? What am I supposed to be doing that I'm not? Why don't you punish me instead of taking away the people I love?" before ending, once again, with the sentiment, "You prick!" The chapel scene revealed part of Andy's character—his fear of and reverence for God. After venting his feelings honestly to God, he turned around and tenderly asked for His help.

There comes a point in many people's spiritual journey where their idea of God, the ideas that make up their faith, have to be broken down and reexamined. Usually these "dark nights of the soul," as the mystic St. John of the Cross called them, come in the form of some tragedy, spiritual or otherwise, when their faith is truly tested.

Often, if God or spirituality is presented on a television show, God is depicted as some sort of cosmic genie (or capricious child), or a person's spiritual walk is seen as either saccharinely naïve or their faith completely absent. It is rare to see a true grappling with faith or the reality of God.

When God wants to enter someone's life—take them to a newer, deeper understanding of Him or otherwise get their attention—it is, more often than not, quite painful. Andy Sipowicz does what too few of even the most "spiritually"-minded people do: hold on. His faith isn't pretty; his words aren't the practiced reverence that we've come to imagine holiness should look like, but they are real. He has learned that true faith is not without hardships and there aren't pat answers to one's questions. There is mystery that will either break someone and cause him to

abandon God, or it will draw him closer to Him. Faith is about persever-
ance; Andy persevered and came out the better man for it.

*Maurice Broaddus holds a bachelors of science degree in Biol-
ogy (with an undeclared major in English) from Purdue University and works as an environmental toxicologist. He has been
involved in ministry work for well over a decade and is in the
process of becoming a pastor and planting a church. His horror fiction has been published in numerous magazines and Web
sites. His television reviews can be read at the Hollywood Jesus
Web site (www.HollywoodJesus.com). He is married to the lovely
Sally Jo and enjoys life with two sons, Reese and Malcolm. Learn
more at www.MauriceBroaddus.com.*

DAVID BRUCE

What Would the *Blue* Do?: *NYPD Blue* From a Spiritual Point of View

Behind the harsh language and nudity of NYPD Blue *lies some-thing no one expected.* Bruce explains why NYPD Blue *is the most spiritual show on television.*

MOST PEOPLE DON'T THINK of *NYPD Blue* as a television show that underscores important spiritual values—but surprisingly it does. Consider this: The members of the 15th Precinct genuinely care for each other and are devoted to their common pursuit of justice, confronting evil and protecting human life. In spiritual terms this critically acclaimed series is about fellowship, self-sacrifice, integrity, community and commitment. That's strong spiritual stuff!

Not surprisingly, however, religious people are often the last ones to recognize basic spirituality. Three months before *Blue* was to debut on ABC, moral watchdog and rock thrower Rev. Donald Widmon, an ordained minister of the Untied Methodist Church and founder of the American Family Association (AFA) led a national campaign against *NYPD Blue*. He called on affiliates not to air the program and organized citizens to boycott products advertised during the show. He had tremendous results—a quarter of ABC's 225 member stations preempted the first episode, even after the show's producer caved in and trimmed fifteen seconds from the sex scene. Things were looking grim.

Reverend Widmon was on a campaign to save America from the so-called evils of the *Blue*, and he took his campaign seriously. As he often recounts, one evening in 1977 he sat down to surf the channels for something his family could watch together. "On one channel was adultery," he says, "on another cursing, on another a man beating another over the head with a hammer. I asked the children to turn off the TV. I sat there, got angry, and said 'They're going to bring this into my home, and I'm going to do all I can to change it.'"

After brooding for a while he came up with a campaign for his church to turn off the TV for a week. He then went public with his idea, sending out a press release which the national media picked up. Through subsequent publicity he established a membership list of thousands who felt the same way he did. Thus the American Family Association came into being.

Widmon and the AFA had *NYPD Blue* in their cross hairs; the goal was to keep it off the air. The campaign was effective, but not effective enough. Despite the unprecedented number of affiliates that didn't air the first show—a situation that would have doomed most other shows—*NYPD Blue* scored amazingly well in the ratings. Widmon's campaign had an interesting reverse effect; it provided awareness and publicity. The public was ready for something new and different on television—not only did they tune in, but also they returned week after week, giving the show legs. The advertisers and affiliates ceased their opposition. By the close of its first season it won endorsements from Viewers for Quality Television and the People's Choice and Emmy awards, not to mention accolades from the majority of television reviewers.

Even though *NYPD Blue* will forever be known for its part in pushing broadcast TV into new terrain with its partial nudity, language, violence and sex, viewers find something more than all that, something spiritual they connect with in a profound way.

NYPD Blue doesn't balk at controversial language. Without being racy or exploitive, it has never compromised the understanding that culture lives in language. ABC even provides a cautionary statement to advise the viewer of the show's verisimilitude: "This police drama contains adult language and scenes with partial nudity. Viewer discretion is advised."

Christian scriptures present God as always communicating in the language of the culture. In the book of Acts the followers of Jesus were given the gift of "tongues" on the Day of Pentecost, enabling them to speak in the languages of the various groups gathered in Jerusalem.

NYPD Blue blesses broadcast television with the gift of "tongues"—enabling it to better speak in the language of the culture.

"Sex is a very holy subject."
—GEDDES MACGREGOR

NYPD Blue presents responsible sexuality that's rooted in caring and committed relationships. It has repeatedly celebrated sexuality within the context of loving human relationships. Conversely, it cautions against the dark side of sexuality, which is devoid of human compassion. Numerous episodes have dealt with the evil and pain of rape and sexual abuse. The show balances its portrayal of sexual perversity with story arcs that celebrate the goodness of sex in loving, committed relationships. According to the Hebrew scriptures God created humans as sexual beings, and declared this human connection to be "very good."

NYPD Blue has always striven for the kind of integrity Plato spoke of when he said, "I would rather that the whole world should be at odds with me, and oppose me, than that I myself should be at odds with myself and contradict myself."

NYPD Blue has integrity because it pursues an honest portrayal of the world it reflects. This sophisticated adult police drama is responsible; the sexual content is never licentious.

Some accuse the show of gratuitous violence, but these charges have never found substantial ground. *NYPD Blue* never exploits violence and rarely depicts violent acts—rather it focuses on the terrible consequences of such actions. The writers hold our attention while at the same time being socially responsible. Their work has become a model for other crime drama shows such as the incredibly popular *CSI: Crime Scene Investigation* series and spin-offs (*NYPD Blue* alums David Caruso and Kim Delaney star as crime scene investigators on *CSI: Miami*). *NYPD Blue* was the pioneer!

Pope John Paul II said, "Violence is a crime against humanity, for it destroys the very fabric of society." Violence is the very "crime against humanity" that *NYPD Blue* fights. The show ultimately reveals a commitment to justice.

I like to think that the realistic treatment of violence in *NYPD Blue* has contributed in some way to the historic decline of violence. America had the highest murder rate of any industrial nation for a solid 100 years before television and 120 solid years before R-rated movies. Starting at the about the same time as the 1993 television premiere of *NYPD Blue* violence took a major decline.

While there is a widespread public perception that crime rates have skyrocketed, the reality is that from 1970 to 1994, violent crime rates remained remarkably stable. Since 1994, violent crime has fallen. In fact, according to the U.S. Department of Justice, violent crime in 2003 was at its lowest level ever recorded. In the past thirty years, the murder rate has *not* steadily increased. In fact, the murder rate in the United States is at the lowest level it has been since 1966.[8]

The U.S. Department of Justice Bureau of Justice Statistics publishes crime statistics on yearly bases. A simple visit to its Web site (http://www.ojp.usdoj.gov/bjs/glance/tables/viortrdtab.htm) reveals the amazing downturn in crime and violence:

National Crime Victimization Survey
Violent Crime Trends, 1973–2003

Adjusted violent victimization rates
Number of victimizations per 1,000 population age 12 and over

Year	Total violent crime	Murder	Rape	Robbery	Aggravated assault	Simple assault
1973	47.7	0.1	2.5	6.7	12.5	25.9
2003	22.3	0.1	0.5	2.5	4.6	14.6

"There are some men and women in whose company we are always at our best. All the best stops in our nature are drawn out, and we find a music in our souls never felt before."
—WILLIAM HENRY DRUMMOND

Each episode of *NYPD Blue* conveys the soul music of community. True to this assessment, it features complicated human characters, none of whom are one-dimensional. Each member is flawed and in every way human—not at all like the ever-perfect Sgt. Joe Friday of the classic *Dragnet* series. The motley crew of characters in *Blue* form a tight-knit (if dysfunctional) community.

An old Jewish proverb states that "the world is a collection of cogs; each depends on the other." Such a collection of interconnecting cogs

---

[8] BJS homicide rate trends, <http://www.ojp.usdoj.gov/bjs/glance/tables/hmrttab.htm> viewed September 28, 2004.

is at the heart of the 15th Precinct, where the officers genuinely care for each other and devote themselves to the common pursuits of upholding justice, confronting evil and protecting human life.

In June of 1999 CNN aired an eye-opening ten-minute news piece called *Prime Time Prophets* which presented *NYPD Blue* as leading the way in a new cultural understanding of spirituality. The producer and writer, award-winning broadcast journalist and documentarian Silvia Gambardella, spoke of the spiritual aspects of *Law & Order* and *NYPD Blue* which led her to make the well-received piece: "I used to be a crime reporter, which is why I love these shows to begin with. With all the attacks they've been getting, I started to see other things in them, solely as a viewer, scenes about God and the Bible and spirituality and family values in shows where you wouldn't expect it."

In 1999 one would expect such spirituality in obvious shows such as *7th Heaven* and *Touched by an Angel*, "But not in *Law & Order* and *NYPD Blue*."

Gambardella, a Catholic, observed the frequency of spiritual themes in *NYPD Blue*. For example, she noted spiritual metaphors in the "Hearts and Souls" episode of the dying Bobby Simone and the award-winning episode "Lost Israel," in which Sipowicz solved a murder with clues from Bible passages given to him by a homeless man.

Gambardella said of the deeply flawed Sipowicz character: "What's incredible is how much this man has traveled in his own spiritual journey. Nobody is like (the angels on) *Touched by an Angel*, but we all can identify with some part of Sipowicz because he's so human."

What is interesting about the difference between *Touched by an Angel* and *NYPD Blue* is that the latter outlived the former. The culture has moved from a *Precious Moments* G-rated spirituality to an R-rated *The Passion of the Christ* type.

No episode demonstrates the spiritual center of the show better than the award-winning "Hearts and Souls." Millions tuned in as the beloved Det. Bobby Simone struggled for survival after a heart transplant. This particular show underlined the spiritual values of inner struggle, committed friendship, self-sacrifice, integrity, community and the very value of life itself.

After Simone received the heart transplant, he laid in his hospital room with his wife, Det. Diane Russell, at his side. The members of the 15th Precinct crowded into the hospital waiting room to witness their dear friend being released. The depth of their compassion could not have been more obvious. In my mind, this kind of commitment and devotion to others is what true spirituality should always exemplify.

Everything was going as well as could be expected as Bobby proclaimed anxiously, "If I don't get out of here now, I may never leave." He was hopeful to the very end.

As Diane buttoned his shirt, she noticed a little yellow drainage coming out of the bandages. It was a paralyzing moment as they both realized what this meant: life-threatening infection. The Bible speaks of death as the final enemy of life.

The CAT scan revealed that Bobby had an aggressive infection in his chest cavity, which spread to other parts of his body, including his brain. As a last-ditch effort, they placed him on antibiotics.

The 15th reconvened at Diane's request and they all sensed her meaning.

Bobby, feverish and delirious, recounted his professional successes as a police officer. He began to look forward to meeting the daughter he and Diane had lost to miscarriage in the hereafter. This was a precious moment that underscores the human hope for happiness in an afterlife.

As Sipowicz and the other detectives came by to say their final farewells, Bobby made the gesture of surrender—he was ready to go. Diane took the ring from his finger, placing it on her own as Bobby passed into the next life. A powerful scene of profound spirituality at its most human level.

Over a quarter century ago a Roman Catholic priest established the Humanitas Prize for the purpose of encouraging Hollywood writers to explore the best instincts of the human spirit. *NYPD Blue* won the award in 1999 for "Hearts and Souls." Upon receiving the award on behalf of the *NYPD Blue* team David Milch explained that while his writing had always explored human values and dignity, winning the Humanitas Prize "has raised the bar" for him, encouraging him to reach higher in his spiritual journey.

In summary he stated, "I'm grateful to have lived long enough now to have come to believe that the shadow—in which I believe I must inevitably reside, as well as all of my characters—is cast by God's protective hand."

Milch, a former Yale professor, wrote for *Hill Street Blues* before cocreating *NYPD Blue* with Steven Bochco. These credentials are qualification enough to be a writer for the show, but the human depth that is so evident in his writing comes from a different place. It is said that creativity often comes out of chaos, and according to Milch he has been fight-

WHAT WOULD THE BLUE DO? • 135

ing inner demons for years. He suffered through major heart surgery and fought off drug addiction earlier in his life. Those inner spiritual battles show up in episodes of *NYPD Blue*. He once said, "When I'm in my head, I'm in a very bad neighborhood."

Milch makes a point of being aware and open about the spiritual quality of his work. At a 2001 writing seminar, 300 people gathered to learn about writing from him. Brian Lowry was one of those who attended. He summarized that "Milch's presentation is a multifaceted experience—part one-man stage show, part meditation on world events, part evangelical revival (he reads from the Bible occasionally to illustrate points about drama) and, perhaps most of all, part graduate-level psychology course."

Milch demonstrated the value of struggling and overcoming inner demons; *NYPD Blue* owes a great deal of its success to his spiritual struggle. No character in *NYPD Blue* mirrors that struggle better than Sipowicz.

None of the members of the 15th are 100 percent righteous. They are flawed humans, just as all of us are, and yet they are committed to making the world a better place. The depiction of the human situation is both honest and hopeful. *NYPD Blue* connects us to the realities of the world in which we live and yet delivers a sense of hope that we can make a difference.

Additionally *NYPD Blue* constantly reminds us that the hardest work we will do is with ourselves—just as Andy has had to do with his battles to overcome the bottle. When Andy's wife died—the sort of trauma, which, in the past, had sent Andy back to the bottle—it did not conquer him. He had overcome. He was a changed man. The message here is: we can overcome our demons!

NYPD Blue speaks to that hope for redemption and renewal in all of us. Hope is what the *Blue* is all about.

David Bruce is a film critic with a background in both television and theology. He is founder of the popular hollywoodjesus. com, which views popular culture from a spiritual point of view. He has served as an administrator for NBC in California, received his masters of divinity degree from North Park University Seminary in Chicago and has pastored three churches. He travels extensively, speaking at schools, conferences and churches. He currently resides with his family in southern Oregon.

ELLEN KIRSCHMAN

Bare Butts, Bare Souls: The Occupational Hazards of Relationships in *NYPD Blue*

NYPD Blue shows us police detectives at home, with their husbands and wives, with their children. It shows police officers making mistakes and being human, and reveals how being on the job impacts being a lover, a husband and a parent. According to police psychologist Ellen Kirschman, the show usually gets it right.

PEOPLE DON'T USUALLY PICTURE police officers in a family context. More often we think of them as macho, one-dimensional, door-kicking, rugged individualists with few family ties—a characterization that prevents us from considering them as humans living out their lives as real people with real problems—marriages, mortgages, children, addictions and aging bodies.

The first television show to portray cops as real people was *Police Story; Hill Street Blues* continued to explore the spaces behind and beside the badge with stories showing the complex interaction of the personal and the professional. In every episode cops were allowed the full range of human emotion.

NYPD Blue stepped into the breach six years later. *Hill Street Blues* creators David Milch and Steven Bochco once again created believable characters whose lives and struggles have an enduring and compelling truth. This is not to say that the series doesn't occasionally fall victim to sexist, action-junkie Hollywood-style scripts or that its appeal doesn't wax and wane with various actors—but the flawed and bumbling characters and troubled relationships mirror the real world in which many cops live. As a police psychologist, it is a world with which I am very familiar.

NYPD Blue has broadened our understanding by featuring a wide range of family situations. Some episodes reveal how family histories can affect the choice to be a police officer in the first place. Others show how officers' families can buffer the stress of the job or add to it. Still others demonstrate how police training influences and changes the way cops relate to the people they love. Most always the emphasis is on the dramatic. In the real world there are plenty of normal cops from normal families.

Don't Take Your Training Home with You

The skills of a good street cop can interfere with what it takes to be a good spouse, a good lover, a good parent and a good friend. Cops are taught to always appear to be in control of themselves and of the situation. They don't show fear or weakness to suspects. They don't show sadness at a death notification because their presence is meant to stabilize the crisis, they don't tell a child molester they are repulsed by his actions if they expect him to confess, and they rarely show emotions like fear or uncertainty to each other—in the world of policing such emotions signal doubt and hesitancy. This spells trouble in an emergency.

Take Connie McDowell. This beautiful, loveable, sensitive woman grieved for years over the daughter she gave up for adoption. When she finally located the girl, a teenager who was the same age Connie was when she got pregnant, Connie caught her smoking dope and arrested her. She acted like a cop instead of a parent; she investigated and interrogated rather than communicating. Her overbearing actions doomed their reconciliation from the start.

Though Connie was one of the most interpersonally skilled and psychologically savvy people in the squad, she fell back into the familiar territory of being an authority figure when under intense emotional pressure. She couldn't reveal the depth of her sadness and concern and subsequently jeopardized her relationship with her daughter.

Most cops see more pain and misery in the first few years of their careers than the rest of us see in a lifetime. They learn firsthand how vulnerable people are to random violence, especially children. It's difficult to blame Connie for overreacting to her daughter's marijuana smoking when she's seen what can happen to kids who use drugs.

Knowing too much is a real problem for cops. Their jobs require them to be so immersed in the awful things people do to each other that they can, if they're not careful, overprotect the people they love to the point of stifling them and creating resentment. The protective instinct parents have toward their children is intensified for cops because they are sworn and trained to protect and serve. Police officers expect to keep their families safe and to solve problems that come up at home just as they do every day at work. What they sometimes forget is that they need different means to exert influence in their private lives. They can't demand compliance at home the way they can on the street. It's inappropriate and ineffective to use control tactics with one's family. Families don't accept being spoken to like "perps," nor should they. They are not trained to give or take orders and they aren't accustomed to aggressive behavior. Sometimes police officers forget this.

Self-inflation (thinking you know more than anyone else) is an occupational hazard for police officers. Families don't appreciate being told they are naïve. Police officers sometimes forget that what they know is based on a narrow sample of humanity. To assume all teenagers are juvenile delinquents is an error in logic. Still, it is easy to see how cops become suspicious and wary of people; people lie to them almost all the time, even upstanding citizens. As a result, they learn to trust no one as a way to protect themselves and their families.

When I give workshops for police families I put them through a little exercise. I give them a ten-point scale measuring the escalation of force. One represents standard verbal interaction and ten equals deadly force. When I ask what number yelling would rate, cops invariably give it a two or a three. Family members give it a six.

The story about John Clark, Sr., and his son is a particularly extreme example of self-inflation and hypervigilance. This father's arrogance was so great that he didn't trust his grown son to make decisions on his own. It's a myth, of course, that the senior Clark was in charge of his family. Like other children of alcoholics, Junior took the role of family caretaker. It's not an uncommon family dynamic. Most children of alcoholics try to bring order and stability into their homes by filling in for parents who are absent, as in Danny Sorenson's case, or coping with familial dysfunction, as in Diane Russell's family.

For years, Det. Diane Russell rescued her mother from her brutal alcoholic father. Behind the tough cop mask lives a vulnerable, frightened women who drinks too much, can't ask for help and has major trust issues and difficulty getting close to men. She heals herself with help from Andy Sipowicz and Bobby Simone, though it takes some powerful persuasion by Bobby Simone before she agrees to marry him. Despite her troubles, Diane is a good detective. Her choice of career gives her repeated opportunities to exert control over her existence and compensate for a chaotic and damaging family life.

John Clark, Jr., also had difficulty giving up his role as family caretaker. When he was implicated in the death of a prostitute, he realized that his father had been involved with her. Acting upon reflexive response, he covered for his dad and took the blame. This might have been an admirable thing to do, were his father not such a controlling, self-centered troublemaker.

John, Sr., readily agreed to let his son take the heat under the conditions that he would tell the truth if things got too rough. For all his street smarts, he was clueless about how much his son's loyalty was getting him in serious hot water. Junior had to defend himself to his squad mates and others in his precinct; he and his lover Rita were fighting over his decision to sacrifice himself to protect his father. Plus the IAB hounded him, especially Lieutenant Fraker who literally blackmailed Junior to get at Andy Sipowicz. The deal? If Junior would roll over on Sipowicz, Fraker would let him walk on the prostitute's murder. When Junior refused to cooperate, he was put on administrative leave.

Sipowicz, the "good parent" in this episode, had a long-standing animosity toward Clark, Sr., and couldn't stand watching Junior throw his career away for a no-good father. When Andy confronted the senior Clark, he told him just how much trouble Junior was in and challenged him to take responsibility for his own actions. He did just that, and Junior was reinstated. His father barely got a slap on the hand from the IAB (although we later learned he was forced to become an IAB informant).

Unfortunately, the Clark family's troubles were not over. Weeks later when Junior dragged his drunk and obstreperous father out of a bar, he tried to confront his father about drinking and was rebuffed. John, Sr.'s rationale for drinking was that he was working through the humiliation of exposing himself as a "whore monger." He didn't seem to ever recognize how much his behavior hurt and embarrassed his son.

As a final "act of love," John, Sr., decided to get out of Junior's life by killing himself. He left behind a video tape telling his son that he was proud of him, but since his wife died life was not worth living and his job as a father was done.

It was a devastating legacy. Plagued by survivor's guilt, Junior faulted himself harshly for not recognizing earlier that his father was deeply troubled and in need of help. Fortunately, he also learned that being an adult means you have to set boundaries and limits for yourself and for others, even your parents.

We see how he changed when he later became involved in a murder case involving two married police officers. This time he didn't wait around, make excuses or hesitate to take action on his suspicion that the husband was physically and emotionally abusive. Ignoring any fear that other cops would call him a "rat," he telephoned the "early intervention" staff who removed the officer from duty and took his gun. When the officer later attacked his wife with a baseball bat—the only weapon he had—she shot and wounded him in self-defense. Junior's swift action saved her life.

Cops and Domestic Violence

It was brave and right-minded of the producers and writers to expose the issue of domestic violence in police families. Police psychologists and victims' advocates agree that this is a serious concern, although we often differ on the size and the causes of the problem. Victims and their advocates are adamant that police officers are among the worst abusers and their victims are among the most endangered. Why? Because cops have guns and know how to use them; they're accustomed to using verbal and physical force or the threat of it to get compliance; they know how the legal system works. They also know how to track down missing persons, and their wives can't hide because they often know the locations of the battered women's shelters. Occasionally officers may cover for each other or compromise their objectivity when called upon to investigate or report their friends.

This came up in a recent episode. John, Jr., and Sipowicz suspected the newest detective on their squad of stalking an ex-girlfriend and having killed his wife as she was about to leave him (the murder was blamed on gang violence). Though the other officers were reluctant to pursue this possibility, Sipowicz adamantly refused to look the other way.

Romance in "The House"

Besides raising the shameful issue of domestic abuse in police families, the show reveals the hazards and complications of on-the-job intimacy.

There are a lot of office romances on *NYPD Blue*, so many, in fact, that it makes police work look positively incestuous. With few exceptions, only Lieutenant Fancy, Greg Medavoy and Andy Sipowicz have stay-at-home spouses or wives who don't work in law enforcement.

Apparently "ordinary" police families don't lead dramatic enough lives to have featured roles. After all, what's interesting about domestic chores, childcare problems, financial pressures and communication difficulties? Still, I wonder—with whom did Mrs. Medavoy have an affair and what finally prompted her to give Greg the boot? How is Mrs. Fancy after her miscarriage, her perilous pregnancy and her troubles raising a foster son? And what became of Lieutenant Bass's wife? The poor woman was so tired of playing second fiddle to the job that she set herself on fire just to get her husband's attention.

This emphasis on office romances is a bit theatrical. In real life, most departments frown on nepotism and "fraternizing" between officers, particularly those of different ranks. Known couples are usually assigned to different shifts in different units. The same attitude prevails regarding relationships with other law enforcement professionals, like dispatchers. Everything a police officer does, even in his or her private life, can have unexpected or unintended ramifications. Andy Sipowicz's and Baldwin Jones' affairs with district attorneys were particularly perilous choices that could have potentially compromised the outcomes of cases they were working on together.

Bobby Simone and reporter Benita Alden had an unusual relationship, given that cops generally distrust the media. In an unguarded moment following a sexually intimate encounter, Bobby told Benita about a case involving a cop who murdered a pimp. It was being investigated in utmost secrecy to avoid embarrassing the officer's wife and children.

The next morning the case made front-page headlines in Benita's newspaper and the accused officer killed himself. Bobby, overwhelmed with guilt, felt like he personally put the bullet through the dead officer's brain. When he confronted Benita, who denied she leaked information to the reporter, she got angry at Bobby's interrogation. He was unwilling to do anything but question her truthfulness and she finally stopped denying any complicity because no matter what she said Bobby wouldn't believe her. Despite his treating her like a suspect instead of his lover, she was willing to try and work on their relationship. Bobby was not. His mind was made up.

Bobby's interaction with Benita confirms a truth to which Bobby and many cops subscribe: be on guard because everyone has a hidden agenda. Such wariness creates a self-protective barrier that few can penetrate.

The list of office romances on *NYPD Blue* reads like a fluctuating duty roster. Couples change frequently, moving in and out of each other's lives and beds with ease: Sylvia and Andy, Andy and Connie, Bobby and Diane, Diane and Danny, Danny and Mary, Greg and Donna, James and Gina, John Clark, Jr., and Rita, Rita and Rodriquez, Laura and John, John and Janice, Baldwin and Valerie, Don and Jill ... and this is not the whole list.

There *are* distinct advantages to being in a relationship with another police officer. For one thing, cops are trained alike and understand each other's work. They know most of the players in the office politics. They can counsel each other on career moves, talk through stressful issues and be a source of both emotional and practical support.

Positive examples of office romances can certainly be found on *NYPD Blue*. Diane stood by Bobby through his illness. Sylvia got Andy off the sauce. Mary tried to help Danny with the nightmares he had about his family. Rita stuck with John Clark, Jr., when he was being investigated for his father's behavior. At great peril to himself and his career, John Kelly tried to help his lover Janice with her dysfunctional, "mobbed-up" family. James Martinez did the right thing by Gina when she got pregnant and when she was disfigured in a knife attack. Baldwin Jones supported ADA Valerie Haywood when she was being pursued by a stalker. Connie eagerly helped Andy with childcare for Theo and did an incredible job of soothing and calming his turbulent moods.

Andy Sipowicz deserves special mention. He certainly let the women in his life down at times, especially his ex-wife Katie. But once he stopped drinking and got over his intimacy issues, he turned a corner for the good. He was there for his wife Sylvia when she believed a teenager had been wrongly sentenced to jail. He helped Connie deal with the daughter she gave up for adoption and stuck with her even when she didn't follow his advice. He supported her emotionally when her sister was beaten and later killed by her husband. When Connie wanted to adopt her dead sister's baby, Andy stood by her, fought for her and risked his reputation for her.

The negative consequences of cops coupling are equally abundant. They live their lives in fishbowls, where everyone knows their business.

Rita continually faced coming to work and facing her ex-lover John Clark, Jr. It was painful for her to listen to him talking to his new girlfriend on the office phone. The same goes for Baldwin and Valerie, who continued to work together after she became pregnant and lost their child under somewhat mysterious circumstances. He seemed ready to settle down and create the family he never had, but she sensed that he was motivated by all the wrong reasons. Day after day, episode after episode, they tiptoed around each other trying unsuccessfully to hide their anger and disappointment from everyone in the unit.

Law enforcement couples also fall victim to the tendency to lose their outside friends and spend most of their time together talking about work. When one of them gets in trouble, the other may feel defensive or guilty by association. Jill and Don Kirkendall are a prime, though extreme, example. His illegal behavior, including kidnapping their son, put several officers in jeopardy and nearly ruined Jill's entire life, eventually forcing her to leave the job and her friends.

In the real world, there are reasons cop couples rarely, if ever, work together. One of them is safety. In a crisis, emotions can trump objectivity and common sense. Men in particular are prone to be overprotective when their female companions are in jeopardy. Jimmy couldn't stand it when Diane was undercover romancing a dangerous drug dealer. It forced him to take unwarranted risks. His overprotectiveness caused tension at home and insulted Diane's competence as an officer. Danny made the same mistake when he interfered with Diane's cases and actually followed her on the job, and Baldwin took some illegal steps when Valerie asked him to protect her from a violent criminal defendant who was stalking her.

Romance in this workplace causes more relational and vocational complications than in a traditional office. Though the show doesn't mimic reality in this aspect, office romance in *NYPD Blue* is a key plot device. The show wouldn't be the same without it.

Realistic Characters and Situations

When *NYPD Blue* aired in 1993 it was billed as TV's first primetime R-rated series because it contained nudity, profane language and graphic sex. After ten years the on-screen warning about adult content still flashes before each opening scene, although the show itself now seems tame in comparison to what we can see on HBO or MTV. What's kept our interest over all these years is not bare butts, but bare souls. The characters on *NYPD Blue* are as complex and flawed as they are brave and beautiful. Their reactions are unpredictable and change with time and experience. Like the real cops I know they struggle to stay interested and involved in work. They fight to maintain their humanity and humor in spite of the relentless onslaught of misery and depravity that is their daily fare. They protect each other from the bad guys as vigorously as they band together against a heartless and suffocating bureaucracy. When they regularly break rules, often without the consequences real cops face, we love them for it because their ferocity is softened by familiarity.

How can we be angry at Sipowicz's badge-heavy interrogation techniques when we know how much loss and pain he has suffered in his private life? How can we excoriate him for cutting legal corners when we see how tender he is toward Theo, toward Connie, toward his tropical fish?

This is what makes *NYPD Blue* work. By refusing to lapse into mindless stereotypes, the series offers viewers a behind-the-scenes, play-within-a-play glimpse at how challenging it is for police officers to reconcile their personal and professional lives. If things are this difficult for characters in a TV show, there can be little doubt left about how hard real cops strive to create or preserve a private family life uncontaminated by their jobs.

Ellen Kirschman, Ph.D., police and public safety psychologist, is the author of I Love a Cop: What Police Families Need to Know *(Guilford, 1997) and* I Love a Firefighter: What the Family Needs to Know *(Guilford, 2004). She lives in California.*

JOY DAVIDSON

Fearless Femmes or Wanton Women?: The Trouble with Mainstream Moralism in *NYPD Blue*

Dominatrices. Incest. Crushing fetish. Autoerotic asphyxiation. Not to mention lots of casual sex. So it would seem NYPD Blue *is really pushing the envelop on cutting-edge sexuality. Psychologist and sex therapist Davidson explains why appearances may be deceiving.*

SEASON AFTER SEASON, *NYPD Blue* has nabbed awards for its gritty backstreet plots, stellar acting and giddy backside camera action. When the show premiered in 1993, its strong language, clever dialogue and derrieres both saggy and taut brought rough-hewn realism to the small screen. But what was courageous then seems oddly conventional now, especially with erotic extravagance a full-frontal staple of cable TV serials.

NYPD Blue still offers up a dizzying array of sexual twists and intertwining relationships, ever whirling around the flinty vulnerability of Det. Andy Sipowicz. Convoluted crimes *du jour* highlight the passions of the presumably Lower East Side neighborhood, a locale that has transformed as much as any other recurring cast member over the show's run. Tenements rub shoulders with gentrified brownstones; anxious DINKs[9], their designer pooper-scoopers held at attention, prom-

---

[9] DINK = couples with Dual Income, No Kids

enade pedigreed pups in stride with blue-collar mutts. It's obvious that the 15th covers one of the most diversely cosmopolitan communities in the world, yet, within the precinct, prosaically traditional values reign. While the weekly influx of criminal cases has introduced to Middle America the most novel erotic tastes—sadomasochism, autoerotic asphyxiation and "crushing" fetishes, for example—nearly every overture takes place within an atmosphere of judgment and aspersion, and folks who veer beyond white-bread sexuality are usually presumed guilty until proven just plain disgusting.

In this respect, *NYPD Blue* has pushed boundaries with less-than-protean flair, faltering in its willingness to challenge stereotypes or taboos and buckling under its own limitations. Sipowicz's worldview seems embedded in the teeming activity of the precinct: his inner life—bloated with bigotry, sexism and hostility (along with noble urges to become a better human being)—is exposed in a kaleidoscopic outer world where drag queens, dominatrices, cheaters, strippers and prostitutes are painted from a nightmarishly garish palette. Andy's biases, and perhaps even his repressed desires, are brought to life through this collection of carnivalesque characters, their uni-dimensionality contrasting starkly with the show's emotionally complex central roles. The women, especially, are treated as cardboard cutouts rather than multifaceted beings.

Reviewers have frequently critiqued the starveling depiction of the female leads within this otherwise rich production. If our favorite "normal" gals are largely foils for more substantial male characters, those on the margins are so narrowly drawn that they actively deflect an audience's serious contemplation of their lives. Reminiscent of characters in 1940s and 1950s *film noir* morality tales, the ill-fated "bad girls" of *NYPD Blue*—that is, girls who just say no to hetero, vanilla or compliant sex—always get their comeuppance.

Two Gals and a Baby

In what began as a funny, tender story arc, Det. Greg Medavoy put the moves on Det. Abby Sullivan only to discover that she was already committed to her girlfriend, Kathy. Greg and Abby carved out a friendship anyway, and one day she suggested he meet her lover, as they had a matter they wanted to discuss with him. During their first threesome dinner date, Greg tripped all over himself to be likeable and wound up at his bumbling, anxious worst, embarrassingly tongue-tied and inappropriate. ("That picture on the wall—is that a...a vagina?") The ladies shelved their proposition for the moment, but eventually Abby came clean with Greg: she and Kathy wanted a baby, and they wanted him to be the genetic daddy.

If Sipowicz is the hardened, streetwise, dark soul of the show, then Greg Medavoy is his gawky, humble pie alter—all heart, rashes, curiosities and occasional flashes of brave idealism. Greg couldn't say no to Abby, but once he made his contribution, the inevitable tragedy struck. Abby was shot during an apparent robbery, and Kathy was mortally wounded. As it turned out, the crime was actually masterminded by Abby's bitter, rejected ex-girlfriend. Stunned and grief-stricken, Abby was left alone to raise the child that was to be hers and Kathy's.

Abby and Kathy were ordinary gals by most standards—well-rounded, completely sane, leading lawful lives and typifying nothing more subversive than the prospect of a blissful, two-mommies nuclear family. In a fair world, they'd have hung around to bounce grandkids on their aging, knobby knees. But in a *Blue* world, even open closets hold rotting skeletons—in this case, a paranoid homicidal ex—reminding us that very bad things still happen to even good gay girls, and chicks who dare challenge cultural conventions also tempt the fates.

The Devil and Dr. Devlin

When John Clark, Jr., began dating Dr. Jennifer Devlin, audiences were treated to an accomplished and beautiful woman who merrily swigged her sex with a light chaser of kink. One night she tried sneaking into John's apartment and into his bed as he slept—a gender-switch on the classic "intruder" fantasy—but wound up staring down the barrel of a pistol far more lethal than the one she thought would just be glad to see her.

When next they met, the peripatetic vixen had another surprise in store for John. She had purchased a video camera so they could watch their own bedroom antics after the fact. Junior was less than thrilled with her ingenuity and gently explained that performing for posterity was not his idea of a good time. Rebuffed for the second time, the lady left in a huff.

But we hadn't seen the last of Dr. D. Soon after, a flurry of perfumed invitations lured John to a noontime assignation at a Gramercy Park hotel. He showed up late, grumpy about the twenty-minute drive and couldn't seem to shake his annoyance even with a scantily clad Jennifer draped around him like a feather boa, cooing that she'd been a naughty girl who needed to be handcuffed and firmly interrogated. Bathed in candlelight, alone with a gorgeous, firecracker-hot, wildly imaginative and not easily dissuaded beauty—in other words, most men's karmic jackpot—John should have been wondering what he did in another life to merit such a lavish reward. Instead, he was stuffier than a sealed attic at high noon.

The serial, formulaic nature of *NYPD Blue* demands that nasty reversals soon follow upon even flawlessly promising setups, so we expected that either John would have turned out to be missing some male marbles or Jennifer's too-good-to-be-true femme-fatale act would prove more fatal than femme. Sure enough, John's unresponsiveness provoked Jen's violent temper, and she tossed him out of the room. Any woman might have been miffed by his reserve, but Jennifer went so sufficiently bonkers that she finally managed to incite his interest. Later, she confessed her dark secret: she was manic-depressive, and not only had she trashed her libido-chilling mood-meds upon meeting John, she had also started popping uppers, initiating a downward spiral into manic frenzy. Despite failed attempts to stay on her medication, and even with John's support, by the season's conclusion the only bedpost she had managed to get herself tied to was in a psych ward.

Jennifer Devlin's wasn't *NYPD Blue's* first cautionary tale of a troubled eager beaver. Earlier in the series there was Geri Taylor, an SM devotee who developed an obsessive attraction to that stubby bear of a man, that irresistible gal-magnet, Andy Sipowicz.

Crushes and More Crushes

Squad PAA Geri's unreciprocated yen for Andy soon became an embarrassment that he discouraged brusquely. Andy was married, but Geri wasn't his type anyway; she was overly cream-fed, far too brassy—in fact, too much like Andy himself. Except sexually: where Andy was tentative, unsure of himself, Geri was decisive. As a "dominant" in the SM scene, she was accustomed to pushing the limits of desire in the men who—and here's the key point—*consensually* gave themselves over to her. Her predatory behavior toward Andy was by no means the norm among kinky gals, or, for all we know, Geri herself, since SM is all about mutual consent and respect for individual boundaries. In fact, the axiom, "safe, sane and consensual" is the pledge of allegiance in SM circles, making Geri's womanhandling of Andy a true aberration. A distinction between Geri's behavior and responsible kink could have been addressed in these scenes, but the writers seemed to be playing more for humor and contempt than enlightenment.

Understandably, Geri's actions caused Andy grave distress. Even the deceptively benign act of adjusting his shirt collar carried a proprietary tenor that Andy found repellent, and when Geri's harassment extended to flashing her rubber bustier, Andy let her know he'd had enough. Still, she refused to take his "no" seriously, convinced that he was hiding his subterranean attraction to her. Finally, Andy complained to Lieutenant Fancy, who called Geri into his office for a little chat. After admitting that, yes, she did try to entice Andy with remarks about her underwear, she later slathered her crush with contempt: "What a little baby you are; what a little tattletale."

Fancy moved Geri upstairs, out of Andy's way, but in the long *Blue* tradition of scary things happening to kinky girls, she soon had a disturbing reason to seek him out again. Geri found the body of her dear friend Tom hanging by the neck in his Greenwich Village apartment, strapped into elaborate bondage gear complete with restraints, mask and women's spike-heeled boots, a victim of autoerotic asphyxia gone wrong.

Tom's death would have technically been Andy's case, but given his distaste for Geri, Diane Russell and Jill Kirkendall were assigned. The detectives learned that Geri had been Tom's lover and dominant for ten years, but when Diane and Jill asked what happened in his apartment, Geri told them to shut their "pretty-girl holes" and threatened to "lawyer up" if she didn't see Andy. Beyond resenting the attractive detectives, her reasons for wanting to talk to him seemed ill-advised. Surely she was aware of his animosity. Why seek help from the man she has harassed and insulted, unless it was just another misguided excuse to get closer? Or, was she counting on Andy's inherent sense of fairness? If so, she was counting right.

Andy reluctantly agreed to talk with Geri, and as her story unfolded, Geri at last began to court some sympathy. Yes, Geri did help Tom into part of his fetish gear, but he finished the job and proceeded to masturbate without her—not an entirely new chain of events. Over the past few months, Tom had grown more inclined to prefer other women or his own company to Geri's.

Andy learned that Tom and Geri were kindred souls during their lonely high school years, but as time passed their interlocking lives diverged. With this new information, Geri's roguish pursuit of Andy began to make sense: perhaps it was her way of expelling grief or exorcising her self-revulsion, a compensatory effort that utterly failed to push away meaner, murkier truths. Andy finally recognized Geri's sorrow, and in a moment that at least simulated sincerity he murmured, "I'm sorry for your loss." Until this point, Geri's character was played for laughs and for sensation. Finally, she was accorded humanity: the gift of Andy's faint compassion.

Even though the Geri episodes ended with a smattering more heart than they began, they relied for dramatic tension—as did the Jennifer/John scenes—on a woman playing rough with the sort of sexual urgency that thwarts alpha male expectation. Similar to pulp novel wanton women who come to a bad end, Jennifer and Geri, in their perversity, could only be redeemed through anguish: in Jennifer's case, bipolar disorder, and in Geri's, self-loathing and grief. Although their secretly tragic inner lives put them within reach of easy pity, they were still consigned to suffer for their sins.

The mainstay of drama is conflict and crisis—and granted, there would be no plot if not for awful things happening to good people. However, by making carnival freaks of women who exult in their sexuality, the show dodges any responsibility to do battle with archaic mores and repressive taboos—all the juicy stuff that made *Blue* so compelling early on.

Sometimes, challenging repression means mustering respect for otherwise grossly distasteful representations of free expression. In one memorable episode ("Upstairs, Downstairs") the officers learned that a murdered girl had been featured in fetish videos wearing high heels and stomping on earthworms. Greg Medavoy screened the film in disgust, and told Jill Kirkendall that he just didn't get it. (In this case, he's hardly alone.) As members of the squad ogled the tape with fascinated revulsion, Kirkendall suggested that the point "has something to do with feet."

Later, after finding the producer of the videos, Medavoy and Kirkendall confiscated his entire stock, virtually putting him out of business. They seemed to feel that they'd done a public service despite the fact that his operation had nothing to do with the model's death. While their self-appointed censorship was troubling, equally disturbing was the show's co-opting of this fetish for its shock value, undiluted by genuine efforts to explain its bizarre appeal.

Commercialized fetishism was reviled in this story, and girls who gotta have kink were condemned in the Geri and Jennifer arcs—but we ain't seen nothin' yet. *NYPD Blue*'s superficial depictions of sadomasochistic sex and the women who love it became painful to watch in season eleven.

Goddesses and Monsters

After Molly, a "massage therapist," turned up dead, the detectives discovered a hidden "playroom" in her apartment. The space was so glutted with shiny latex and leather accessories, bondage accoutrements and implements of pain and pleasure that it looked more like a kinky discount mart than a dominatrix's domain. This was only the first in a series of exaggerated, off-pitch renditions of the commercial world of "BDSM" (i.e., bondage, discipline, dominance, submission, sadism, masochism). When one of the squad, taking in the display, remarked that there were "some sick puppies out there," the lines reflected not only his character's assumptions, but, given the absence of any contrasting perspective, those of a larger culture unschooled in the psychology of power-play. Instead of offering up fresh insight, the scene merely served the average viewer his own preconceived notions, peppered and warmed like soggy leftovers.

Continuing the investigation, Medavoy and Det. Baldwin Jones visited Molly's former business associate, Paulette. They found her in the middle of a D/S (dominance and submission) scene with one of her slaves, a simpering mousy man in a ghastly wig and French maid's uniform. As they began questioning Paulette, she turned to her slave and barked, "Go clean the toilet with your face!" This line, which might elicit knowing chuckles from serious players who understand the difference between "reality" and comic exaggeration, made a mockery of actual professional dominants, who, despite the perceived oddity of their profession, are indeed professional. A real-life pro-domme would be as likely to remain in role, humiliating a slave, as detectives loom in her doorway as to bring a leather-clad and leashed "sick puppy" to a PTA meeting at her children's school.

Paulette, seeking confirmation of her alibi, demanded, "Slave, where was Goddess at six A.M. this morning?" Medavoy agilely slipped into the alternative universe and inquired of the slave, "You wouldn't have any reason to lie for Goddess, would you?"

As soon as Bernard, the slave, realized that his precious Goddess was being questioned about a murder, he dropped his persona, pulled on his pants and reverted to his other "role," that of real-life criminal attorney. *"Silence!"* he commanded Goddess. And she obeyed. Here the writers reminded audiences that competent, intelligent people do what sometimes looks pretty silly if it gets them off. But it's all a game that can end as quickly as it began.

These lighter moments are soon eroded by the discovery that Molly, the murder victim, was involved in an intense D/S relationship with a male client. When interrogated, the former client revealed that he'd asked Molly out on a "normal" date. She accepted, then charged him anyway. Later, he went to see her and she scornfully called him "the names" (which we can only guess are something the likes of "toilet face") and suddenly "went for her canes," whereupon the client insisted he blacked out and had no memory of the incident. Nevertheless, he was willing to admit that he must have defended himself rather fiercely since Molly wound up dead.

The story rang false to the detectives on investigative grounds, but it should have been suspicious for other reasons, one being that the man was describing a seriously abusive relationship, not a professional one. Molly's behavior was well outside the bounds of business practice, but no distinction was made. Reference to the pathological nature of the relationship was called for here. Instead, viewers were left with the impression that this sort of manipulative behavior is common in commercial SM circles, when it actually deviates dramatically.

Eventually, Jones and Medavoy brought in the man's estranged wife for questioning. She broke down, confessing that she went to see Molly, who she felt had an unnatural hold over her husband, and begged her to let him go. When Molly laughed in her face, she attacked her—after all, "someone had to stop her."

All the characters in this secondary story arc seemed to be plaster castings of disturbed women—from Goddess Paulette, to Molly the abusive domme, to the homicidal codependent wife. And BDSM was cast as the drugged catnip that drove the pathetic pussies up a tree, so that when they finally tumbled, they broke their necks. By avoiding realistic portraits of these women, or risking social interrogation of their fictional universe, *NYPD Blue* contributed in its small but damning way to supporting misogynist undercurrents in our real world.

The show's overall treatment of BDSM is heavy on judgment and light on conceptual understanding. Contrary to the impression given by these scripts, clinical experience and research evidence demonstrate that folks attracted to the full range of BDSM activities are as mentally and emotionally healthy as the "vanilla" population. One expert even suggests that as many as thirty-three percent of people dabble in some form of BDSM or power-play. A few years back, a national magazine polled readers and found that a majority of women sometimes like to be dominated in bed. And last year, upwards of 300,000 attendees—players and voyeurs alike—thronged to the annual San Francisco leatherfest known as the Folsom Street Fair. Perhaps the abundance of kink-related subplots in *NYPD Blue* is a nod to this growing interest in alternative sexuality among mainstream Americans—or perhaps it is merely sensationalism. In any case, the tight moral framework of the show—apparently coded with Sipowicz's DNA and able to evolve only so far as its progenitor can—shuns textual illumination of erotic diversity. Like Andy himself, the series relies on something akin to gut-instinct and scornful disparagement in its treatment of sexual misfits.

The limitations of these depictions are even more obvious when contrasted with those of another hit detective drama, *CSI: Crime Scene Investigation*, a series that spotlights the work of a team of forensic scientists in Las Vegas.

Desire's Domain

In "Slaves of Las Vegas" the body of a woman was found naked in a sandbox. Gil Grissom and his team were called in to determine the cause of death. Due to the whip and ligature marks on the body, they initially assumed that the crime was violent, but soon discovered that the woman had worked at Lady Heather's Dominion, an exclusive SM establishment. The investigators paid her a visit and found "Lady Heather" to be a luminous, refined beauty whose keen intelligence added a hypnotic weave of insight and eroticism to their understanding of activities in her domain.

"What happens here isn't about violence," she assured Grissom. "It's about challenging preconceived notions of Victorian normalcy. Bringing people's fantasies to life. Making them real and acceptable."

"Like the theater?"

"In my experience, Mr. Grissom, some men go to the theater; some men *are* the theater. Either way, what I offer is a chance for submission or control—whichever is required. Sometimes a client doesn't know what he wants until I show him."

And she began to show Grissom.

"I can read anyone who walks through this door and know their desires ... sometimes even before they do. Why do you think I selected china and table linens?" Lady Heather asked, expertly pouring tea from a delicate pot into small cups.

"You like fine things," Grissom suggested.

"Or maybe I knew you'd like them. The same way I know you enjoy most of the superficial trappings of civilization."

Grissom was impressed. "I'm that obvious?"

"Only because you try not to be. You spend your life uncovering what is beneath the surface of civility and acceptable behavior. So it's a release for you to indulge in something like high tea when it seems, if only for a moment, that the world really is civilized."

Grissom was silent. The woman was revealing the true skill of a professional dominant—the ability to read others with precision, sensitivity and respect.

"The most telling thing about anyone is what scares them," she continued. "And I know what you fear more than anything, Mr. Grissom."

"Which is?"

"Being known. You can't accept that I might know what you really desire, because that would mean that I know *you*, something you spend your entire life making sure no one else does."

Unlike Pauline or Molly in *NYPD Blue*, Lady Heather was more goddess archetype than slut stereotype, a perfect blend of intellect and compassion and as fluent quoting Yeats as she was giving voice to her companion's furtive yearnings.

In an Emmy-nominated follow-up episode, the tantalizing hint of attraction between Lady Heather and Grissom was heightened.

"Lady Heather's Box" again revolved around the death of someone in Lady Heather's employ. The context of this inquiry allowed Lady Heather to continue her narrative analysis of the dynamics of consensual BDSM relationships, introducing the concept of "safewords" (that is, the method by which the submissive can call an immediate halt to a scene), and an awareness that the dominant often caters to the submissive's sensual desires, thus giving the submissive a great deal of power.

As Grissom questioned Lady Heather about the case, she wondered aloud if his visit was just a business call.

He confirmed that it was, but that he also valued her insight.

"I'm flattered," she replied, smiling. "But you already seem to know the answers to your questions. You keep me in proximity when I walk away, and when I'm close you watch my lips." She moved near to Grissom and asked, "Are you losing your hearing?" (He was.)

"I'm losing my balance," he said.

"Your sense of self?"

"No. I know who I am."

"Do you?"

Grissom nodded, then almost whispered, "Yes, I do."

Reaching out, he brushed the hair away from her face and she closed her eyes, as if to wholly absorb his touch. When she opened them, Grissom framed her face with both of his hands.

"You can always say stop," he told her.

"So can you."

The scene was more than romantically lush; it was politically provocative. By pairing the ethically self-assured Grissom with the bewitching Lady Heather, *CSI* took a definitive stance in support of the unfettered erotic imagination. Their coupling suggested that consensual power-play and pathological behavior are no more analogous than, say, family love and incest. Grissom's world, where science and civility trump prejudice and impulse, exists in distinct juxtaposition to Sipowicz's.

Redeemed at Last?

Although women who veer toward the spirited side of sexuality usually come to a bad end in *NYPD Blue*, the show made a radical shift in "Old Yeller." Once more the character of Greg Medavoy figured prominently.

When Veronica Lewis reported that an heirloom diamond was missing from her jewelry cache, she asked detectives to gently question her nephew, a former drug user who was temporarily living with her. Maybe...just maybe...he pinched the ring, but she didn't want to hurt his feelings by falsely accusing him. Medavoy, ever the nervous knight, was happy to assist the distressed, aging damsel—a petite woman in her late sixties, blessed with elegant bone structure, long, flowing silvery hair and the carriage of a ballerina. Despite their age difference, Veronica exuded a wispy sensuality that magnetized Medavoy.

Nephew Tim denied taking the ring, but was quick to point out other possible culprits, like the fifty or so young swains Veronica met via personal ads and then invited to join her in celebrations of pleasure. Since her husband's death, Veronica had embraced the practices and intricacies of erotic magick, and although she was no longer seeking a life-partner, she was rejoicing in all the ecstasies life offered. Certain that the men with whom she shared her adventures had stolen nothing from her, either emotionally or tangibly, she willingly supplied their names to the police.

At last, a woman who shatters stereotypes: Veronica's delight in carnal love belied the myth that women of her years are on the down slope of sexual vitality, or must languish on the shadow side of desirability.

Medavoy and Jones checked out her lovers, finding that a few had criminal records. One stunner in his twenties came under scrutiny, and we expected to learn that he used the old broad to get to her spoils. Instead, he grew misty when he spoke of Veronica, like an acolyte lauding the gifts of his teacher. Sex with Veronica, in all its Tantric splendor, was the best of his life. If Medavoy had been intrigued before, he was nearly paralyzed with fascination now.

The investigation failed to turn up any other valid leads, and nephew Tim finally confessed. Disgust for his aunt's "slutting around," coupled with his own emotional impoverishment, seemed like sufficient reason for stealing and pawning her ring. We saw here that scorn and condemnation reveal more about the condemner than the condemned.

Medavoy retrieved Veronica's heirloom, but wrestled with his yearning to move the relationship to another level. Inexpert at the directness that Veronica had perfected, he invited her to meet him for coffee, ostensibly so that he could ask her out. Ask her out to ask her out? Naturally, Veronica saw through his gallant charade and reassured him that they were adults, and could speak their minds.

"Do you want to have sex, Detective?"

With this story the show touched upon something magnificent, something so big that the creators almost (but not quite) redeemed themselves for their otherwise tawdry treatment of unconventional women. By allowing Veronica to revel in erotic bliss without consequence, the story underscored the belief that desire and desirability are interlinked, that youth is about *how* we live, not how long we live, and that a woman can bloom like fragrant night jasmine, decade after decade, rather than wither away.

In the final scene between Veronica and Medavoy we saw their imperfect but agile bodies discretely swathed in bed covers, squirming and bumping and rocking. We saw the fish in Veronica's aquarium swooping and bopping in rhythm to their boffing. And when all the happy quaking ceased, Greg felt free enough to admit his confusion over what happened between them so suddenly and so easily, allowing Veronica to share the gift of her earned wisdom: "Life is about simplicity," she told him. And, simply speaking, she wanted to know. . . .

"Would a young buck like yourself have another go-round in him for an old broad like me?"

"I'll do my best, ma'am," Medavoy promised.

Aw, shucks. What could possibly be sweeter?

Well, I'll tell you what would have been sweeter: a different companion storyline, that's what.

While this story hit all the right notes in challenging constricting memes around older women and sexual self-assertion, it should not go unnoticed that the episode's primary plot revolved around the kidnapping and sadistic abuse of a series of women by a monstrously disturbed couple. In these disharmonious tales, vanilla-flavored sexual liberation was affirmed, while kinky sex was paired with coercion and pathological criminal behavior once again. Lurking in the shadows of meaning—visible only by scanning the measured buildup of kink-unfriendly exposition over the years—was the insistent muddling of healthy BDSM spectacle with dioramas of depravity, degradation and death. The erotic ethic projected by the 15th is unambiguous: good sex is "straight" and "vanilla." Boundaries between pleasurable, consensual power-exchange and abhorrent perversity are so smudged as to be barely discernable.

Why is writing a clear boundary so important? Because everyone with a television knows that people with ordinary sexual styles commit crimes. There are good people and bad people who like to do the most unremarkable wooing and screwing. However, everyone with a television does *not* necessarily know that good, perfectly normal people—as well as a few bad apples—are drawn to kinky sex. They don't know if SMers are more or less likely to abuse their partners, to rape, to kill or to evoke outlandish displays of passion in others. They don't know why they, too, have some of the unusual fantasies they do, or what those fantasies mean. They don't know if they should enjoy them or be frightened by them or avoid thinking about them, like pink elephants. *That* is why I see a problem when a show like *NYPD Blue* flaunts erotic fantasy in the service of crime drama but falls short of backing up its choices with contextually accurate information, or better yet, making even one player a voice of knowledge and understanding about erotic diversity.

NYPD Blue is among the handful of high-quality shows that is, as one reviewer has deemed it, a "bully pulpit for promoting tolerance, open-mindedness and other positive values."[10] In most cases, the show uses this authority with conviction and artistry. However, like its central protagonist, Andy Sipowicz, it has room to grow—a football field's length, if you ask me—and a grave responsibility to do so.

At this very moment, the fanatical Right is poised and aching to squelch sexual freedoms throughout America. Millions of tax dollars have already been spent depriving U.S. teens of accurate sex education, and more funds are reserved for the task of literally erasing all refer-

---

[10] "Feed Me TV: Four Arguments for the Avid Consumption of Television," by Zack Stentz, Alternet, (http://www.alternet.org/story/622/)

ences to non-abstinence protection against HIV and other STIs from the public health system—and, yes, that would mean the disappearance of any mention of condoms from discussion or literature. If the Right has its way, the Internet will also become sterilized; sexually explicit materials, including educational matter, will be removed.

The Right does its insidious work beneath the illusory veil of religious values, protectionism and so-called morality. In this climate, those with the cultural currency to strip away the fictions they pander must do so unflinchingly or risk colluding with them by default. Television is critical narrative territory in the fight for individual rights and freedoms, and entities with the influence and viewership of *NYPD Blue* can't afford the small luxury of reinforcing sexual stereotypes or mocking sexual minorities, even for the sake of riveting, award-winning drama.

Today, television is a battleground. And the team at *NYPD Blue* might be wise to reconsider which side of the field it wants to be on.

Joy Davidson, Ph.D., is a certified sex therapist and licensed marriage and family therapist, with a doctorate in clinical psychology. A veteran writer, with dozens of national magazine articles to her credit, she has also been the relationships and sexuality columnist for Playgirl *magazine,* Men's Fitness *magazine and MSN's* Underwire. *She is the author of* Fearless Sex: Overcome Your Romantic Obsessions and Get the Sex Life You Deserve *(Fairwinds, 2004) and* The Soap Opera Syndrome: The Drive for Drama and Excitement in Women's Lives. *She also cocreated the award-winning video series,* Playboy's Secrets of Making Love to the Same Person Forever, Volumes I and II.

GLENN YEFFETH

Darwin and Sipowicz

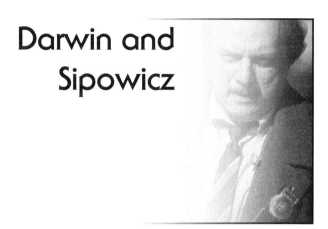

Can't you picture Andy Sipowicz sailing to the Galapagos Islands on the HMS Beagle, *scowling at the finches, collecting new species of fish for his tank, perhaps tuning up the occasional unruly native? No? Then it must just be me.*

WE TAKE THEM FOR GRANTED. The intrepid detectives of *NYPD Blue*, and, more importantly, the real-life police in cities across the world, do a difficult, dangerous and thankless job. It's commonplace to pay lip service to the challenges and risks of police work, and to express gratitude to those who choose to comprise the thin blue line. But why *do* police choose to serve?

NYPD Blue does a excellent job of portraying the dangers and frustrations of life on the force. Police have much higher death and injury rates, from both violent confrontations and accidents, than those in most other professions. Police officers have a higher suicide rate than average; it's common enough to have spawned its own terminology—"eating your gun." And police, while earning respect on the street, do not rate highly in the social hierarchy. In season one of *NYPD Blue* we watched with frustration as Detective Kelly separated from his wife, even as she began a relationship with a doctor in her building. Kelly was keenly aware of the status gap between a NYPD detective and a doctor, and resented it.

In pay, as in social status, police detectives, never mind ordinary police, get the short end of the stick. So why do they do it?

And let's go further. Why do we even need police? The obvious answer is that without police people could commit crimes at will, with no fear of capture or punishment. But this begs the question, why are we so willing to commit crimes? What in our evolution dictated that our collective need to break the rules is so great that we require hundreds of thousands, if not millions, of police around the world? In the words of Rodney King (a good example, incidentally, of why we need police), "Why can't we all just get along?"

These are tough questions. The answers will come from the fascinating and controversial discipline of sociobiology.

Greedy Darwinism

Biology was once the ugly stepchild of the sciences. The hard sciences, physics and chemistry, were about forming increasingly powerful theories to explain the wonders of nature. The hard sciences had a noble mission: to push back the dark territory of the unknown and take mankind closer and closer to an understanding of God's Truth.

Biology, on the other hand, was about finding new bugs and counting their legs. Hard scientists dismissed biologists as glorified librarians, engaged in a never-ending categorization and sorting process, but doing very little to truly expand our insights into the world around us.[11]

All this changed with Darwin and the Theory of Natural Selection. All of a sudden biology had a theory that explained the volumes of facts accumulated over centuries. The painstaking sorting of animals and plants into kingdoms, families and species...suddenly it all made sense. Everything from the shape of birds' beaks to the origins of man now fit into one comprehensive theory. It's difficult to overstate the impact that Darwinism had on biologists—on all educated people—in the late nineteenth century. And that impact continues on into our century.[12]

Philosopher Daniel Dennett calls Darwinism a metaphorical "universal acid," an acid that can eat through any substance. By this he means

---

[11] No offense meant to actual librarians.

[12] I have no objection to those who insist, for religious reasons, that Darwinism is false, just as I have no objection to flat-Earthers or folks who want to make $\pi = 3$ "to keep things simple." But these complaints have nothing to do with science.

that Darwinism repeatedly has proven itself applicable to broader and broader areas of science and philosophy.

In 1975 Edward O. Wilson's monumental work, *Sociobiology: The New Synthesis*, proposed, controversially, that behavior—even human behavior—was a subset of Darwinism. Darwinism had conquered biology, and now it threatened to annex anthropology and sociology, perhaps even psychology. Sociobiology, with its hint of eugenics, was very controversial, but has held up. The debate continues, but few scientists now believe that Darwinian thinking is irrelevant to explaining important aspects of human behavior.

Finally, 146 years after *The Origin of Species*, evolutionary biology has developed sufficiently to take on its greatest challenge: explaining the perps, skels, police and detectives of *NYPD Blue*. And, most ambitiously, explaining the quirky and famously opaque Det. Andy Sipowicz.

A Very Simple Look at a Very Complex Theory

But first, two definitions, starting with Darwinism itself. Darwinism, or natural selection, emerges from consideration of two basic facts of nature.

One, all animals tend to produce far more offspring than will ever make it to adulthood. And of those that do make it to adulthood, not all will successfully find a mate and reproduce.

Second, there is a significant amount of variation within any species, much of which is genetically based and passed on from generation to generation. This variation plays a large role in determining which animals survive and which do not.

Combine these ideas and the result is the theory of natural selection. The animals that breed are the winners; their genetic makeup was better suited to survival and reproduction than those that failed to breed. Therefore the average genetic makeup in the next generation is different from that in the previous generation. The next generation is, infinitesimally, better suited to survive. Over thousands of years, these changes accumulate until the animals, or some subgroup of the animals, have changed dramatically, sometimes becoming an entirely new species. This is what is meant by evolution by natural selection.

Darwinism allows scientists to come up with testable theories about the nature of organisms. Why do giraffes have long necks? Because the giraffes with longer necks ate more and out-competed those with shorter necks. In the next generation, and for generations thereafter, necks became slightly longer, until the cost of having a very long neck overwhelmed the benefits of being able to reach more leaves.

This brings us to our second definition, of sociobiology. Sociobiology posits that this same evolutionary thinking that explains giraffe's necks can also explain their behavior. And can explain the behavior of humans as well. Why do people love to eat sweets? Because in nature, fruit is most nutritious when it is ripe; this is also when it is sweetest. People with genes for eating sweets ate more of the valuable nutrients found in fruit. Our seemingly insatiable appetite for sweets is a legacy from our caveman days, and so, ironically, a behavior that was good for our health in primitive times is quite bad for us now. This sort of irony is common in applying Darwinism to human behavior.

A Caveat

In the High and Far-Off Times the Elephant, O Best Beloved, had no trunk. He had only a blackish, bulgy nose, as big as a boot....

"Come hither, Little One," said the Crocodile, and he wept crocodile tears to show it was quite true. Then the Elephant's Child grew all breathless, and panted, and kneeled down on the bank and said, "You are the very person I have been looking for all these long days. Will you please tell me what you have for dinner?"

"Come hither, Little One," said the Crocodile, "and I'll whisper."
—RUDYARD KIPLING (*Just So Stories*)

Why do men tend to go bald while women rarely do? Because our evolution primarily took place in primitive times, when we were living as hunter-gatherers. Women, as gatherers, spent much more time in the hot sun and needed hair for protection. Therefore women who lost their hair were selected against.

Or because men preferred women with long hair, and bald women had trouble finding mates. Or because the sun gleaming off a bald head allowed men in a hunting party to coordinate their actions at a distance. Or because baldness was considered sexy by those frisky primitive cavewomen.

Some of these explanations are more plausible than others, but all of them are probably nonsense. This illustrates the danger of evolutionary speculation. Evolutionary thinking can make many explanations sound plausible and scientific, but it doesn't make them true. This sort of evolutionary speculation is common, because it's easy and fun to do.

Biologists call these sorts of explanations "just-so stories," in deference to Kipling, but these explanations only become science when backed up by hard evidence.

But that doesn't mean the just-so stories are useless. For one thing, these speculations are the first step in deciding what to collect hard data about. Sometimes the data supports the speculation, and sometimes it leads in fascinating new directions. And, equally important, just-so stories show evolutionary thinking in action. A good just-so story gets the evolutionary principles right and, right or wrong, can be educational for that reason.

We'll be indulging in some just-so stories throughout this essay. Consider yourself warned.

Cooperators and Freeloaders

"Trust, but cut the cards."
—ANONYMOUS

"I tell my wife I'll be home early for dinner."
—DETECTIVE SORENSON, telling a suspect what
he does when he has both participants in a
robbery in custody, implying that a confession
will be soon in coming ("Czech Bouncer")

The Prisoner's Dilemma is a classic puzzle from the mathematics of game theory, and it has important implications for a variety of disciplines, including the evolution of mankind. But for all its subtleties, the setup is quite simple.

Two murderers are captured by the police and interrogated separately. They have been caught red-handed with the stolen goods, but in the absence of any physical evidence of the murder, the most they can get is two years in jail. But, if one squeals on the other, he can get off on a plea-bargain and the other, as they say on *NYPD Blue*, must "face the needle." If they both confess, they can each avoid the death penalty, but they will each face life in prison.

This can be laid out in a simple table, from the point of view either of the prisoners:

		Me	
		Say Nothing	Confess
My Skel Partner	Says Nothing	I get two years in jail He gets two years in jail	I'm a free man He faces the needle
	Confesses	I'm dead man walking He gets off free, the bastard	I get life in the joint He gets life in the joint

This is almost exactly the situation that Sorenson outlines in the quote above, and it comes up quite frequently on *NYPD Blue*. From the point of view of either prisoner, he is better off confessing than not. If his partner confesses, then he's a dead man if he doesn't confess (but only faces life in prison if he does). If his partner doesn't confess, then he gets two years in jail if he doesn't confess (but is a free man if he does). *Whatever his partner does, he's better off if he confesses.*

Let's imagine that both of our prisoners are brilliant and ruthless. They each instantly see the superiority of confessing to staying quiet. So they each confess, and they each wind up spending life behind bars.

Alternatively, let's imagine that our prisoners are dumb but loyal members of a local gang. Each says nothing, and each winds up with only two years in jail. They are far better off than the brilliant and ruthless prisoners.

This may seem like a contrived situation, but we face the Prisoner's Dilemma all the time as individuals or as a society. If my factory pollutes the air, I'm better off, because I save the money it would take to remove the pollutants. But if everyone does this, we're all worse off, choking in filthy air. If caveman Fred hangs back from the hunting party, he's better off—less chance of being gored, and he still gets to eat with everyone else. But if everyone hangs back, the prey escapes and no one eats.

The Prisoner's Dilemma provides a mathematical framework behind a basic fact of life—in many situations, we are individually better off if we look out for ourselves, but we are all better off if we cooperate. This is one of the fundamental issues behind the evolution of behavior, in both animals and man.

Imagine a tribe in which everyone instinctively cooperated with each other. We'll call this tribe, and its individual members, Cooperators. Imagine another tribe in which everyone looked out for themselves. We'll call this tribe, and its members, Freeloaders.

The Cooperators would beat the Freeloaders eight ways from Sunday. They'd be better on the hunt, and better at warfare. They'd out-compete the Freeloaders handily, and wipe them off the face of the Earth. They wouldn't need to waste resources on fences or door locks or chastity belts. Needless to say, the Cooperators would be nothing at all like us.

But why aren't we like the Cooperators, if they are so superior? Why didn't we evolve that way? The reason we didn't is that evolution doesn't work at the tribe level; it works at the individual level. Imagine a Freeloader born into the Cooperator tribe. He would be a fox let into the hen house. He would cheat in every way possible, avoiding work, stealing, sleeping with his neighbor's wife, etc. The Freeloader would out-compete and outbreed his more trusting brethren. Soon Freeloaders would outnumber Cooperators, who would be slowly squeezed out of existence. This is the logic we saw in the Prisoner's Dilemma. Both would be better off if neither cheats, but whoever decides to cheat is better off, especially if the other doesn't!

So the challenge we face, that every social animal species faces, is how to get everyone to act like Cooperators, when we are all better off being Freeloaders. And, if you think about it, we have more or less solved this problem. We all like to freeload when we can, but most of us mostly cooperate, obeying the rules of society even when it's not in our interest to do so.

We've come up with two ways getting cooperation out of our Freeloader natures. The first is straightforward. We set rules for cooperative behavior—limiting polluting, outlawing stealing—and we enforce penalties for breaking these rules. We cooperate because we fear what will happen if we don't. If we don't steal from our bosses, cheat on our wives or snitch on the mob boss, it's to some extent because of our fear of the consequences if we do. In primitive times there were no police, but everyone was alert for rule-breakers, and, no doubt, there were those who made sure punishments were dealt out.

Mankind has evolved to readily spot cheaters in a wide variety of situations. We've gotten very good at reading body language and spotting liars and cheats (although we've also gotten very good at effectively lying and cheating at the same time).

Psychologists have done numerous studies showing how hard-wired we are to detect cheating. For example, consider the following set of playing cards, each of which have a letter on one side and a number on the other[13]:

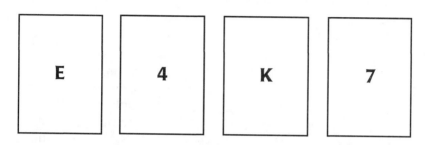

If a card has a vowel on one side, then it must have an even number on the other side, or else the card is defective. Which card(s) do you need to turn over in order to establish that none of the cards is defective? Take a minute and decide the answer.

Now consider this puzzle:

If these cards show age on one side and what the person is drinking on the other, which cards do you need to flip to make sure no one is drinking under age 18? The answer to this one is obvious to most—it's the first and last cards only. You need to flip the Drinking Beer card (to make sure the age is eighteen or over) and the 17 Years Old card (to make sure the drink is non-alcoholic).

The answer to the first puzzle is the same—the first and last cards. This one is a little trickier for most people, *but it's exactly the same problem.* When framed as an abstract puzzle, most people have to think about it and carefully figure it out. When framed as "who's cheating?" the answer is intuitive and almost instantaneous.

---

[13] This comes from Leda Cosmides and John Tooby, "Cognitive Adaptations for Social Exchange," in J. Barkow, L. Cosmides and J.Tooby (Eds.), *The Adapted Mind: Evolutionary Psychology and the Generation of Culture* (Oxford University Press, 1992), pp. 163–228.

Cosmides and Tooby found, through numerous tests, that the ability to spot cheaters was at the heart of our ability to instantly answer some questions, but not others. We have evolved to be very quick to spot cheaters.

We aren't just quick to spot cheaters, but we also have an emotional response to cheating. It makes us angry. When we are being cheated, we seek retaliation, often beyond what is really in our interests. We've evolved this emotional response because it's important to signal to potential cheaters that, if they are caught, the consequences will be significant. Some people have an almost hysterical, over-the-top response to being cheated, going way beyond what is reasonable or even rational. These individuals may have some negative consequences to their extreme overreaction, but, on the other hand, people avoid cheating them. Keep in mind that we evolved in a tribal context, where everyone knew each other, so a reputation for an aggressive response to being cheated was valuable. In game theory this is known as the insanity strategy. If you make it clear that you are insane, no one wants to play chicken with you. Unless, of course, they think you are faking it.

So we cooperate because we're afraid of getting caught if we don't cooperate. But there's a second reason. We've created social institutions that are designed to make us feel that cheating is wrong. Remember, it may be in my interest to cheat, but it's not in my interest for you to cheat. So schools teach the importance of patriotism and teenage gangs preach the importance of loyalty. And the NYPD culture places strong emphasis on never ratting out a fellow cop.

The behaviors we need to have for our own survival and reproduction—collecting and eating food, escaping from danger, having sex as frequently as possible—are rarely praised. The behaviors we want others to have for our mutual benefit—honesty, loyalty, bravery, self-sacrifice—are praised everywhere, from poems to fairly tales. To the extent we can convince each other (if not ourselves) that these attributes are important, the better off society as a whole will be.

But that's not the complete story, because we are *susceptible* to being convinced. We do value patriotism and loyalty and honesty. If it's not in our interests to be these things, then why don't we remain stubbornly selfish?

For one thing, no one likes selfish people. Success today, and even more so in primitive times, lies in convincing your peers, and, more importantly, your superiors, that you are loyal and honest. Remember, we have gotten very good at spotting cheaters, so it's very difficult for someone fundamentally disloyal and dishonest to pose as a boy scout.

So what's the evolutionary solution? To get us to, in fact, value honesty and loyalty.

The cultural indoctrination works because we are primed for it. We do believe in honesty and loyalty and can therefore can project these values to the powers that be. But our evolutionary nature gets it both ways. We value honesty, but when there's a lot at stake we often lie. We value loyalty, but when the tide turns against our team we often turn disloyal. We have evolved to be complex creatures, not even honest with ourselves about how we'll behave.

Darwinism in the Interrogation Room

In *NYPD Blue*, the detectives canvass the streets for witnesses, raid criminal hideouts and even occasionally take on the dreaded Rat Squad. But the really hard work always seems to take place in the interrogation room. Questioning everyone from reluctant witnesses to hardened criminals, Sipowicz and his fellow detectives must determine the best way to get the information they need, even as their interviewee does his or her best evade their efforts. In the interrogation room we occasionally see Sipowicz at his most brutal, but we always see him at his craftiest.

With our primer on Darwinism, we now fully see what the detectives of *NYPD Blue* are up against. Let's consider some of the techniques that the detectives of *NYPD Blue* use, and how they make sense in an evolutionary context:

1. If there are multiple suspects, the detectives always imply that they are each implicating the other. As we have seen, loyalty only extends so far, and we have evolved to anger quickly at even the thought of being cheated. Implying cheating can quickly get a suspect to abandon his sense of loyalty.

2. When Sipowicz is interviewing a witness who seems to be holding back he will quickly get very aggressive, implying that violence is not far off. He'll do this even if the witness is not a suspect. We've evolved to be loyal to our friends, and we've evolved to shed this loyalty quickly when we are in jeopardy.[14] By stimulating the witness's fear response, Sipowicz hopes to shift the witness from loyalty to self-preservation. He often succeeds.

---

[14] I know this sounds cynical, and I recognize and share the respect society gives those individuals whose loyalty remains in the face of great personal risk. We admire these folks because they are rare.

3. Some detectives, Simone for example, will shift into the same street slang as the suspect uses. Others, such as Medavoy, will simulate deep compassion for the suspect. None of this consciously changes their respective positions or interests. But at some level these detectives are indicating that they are of the same tribe as the suspect, increasing his willingness to share information and lowering his guard.

4. When trying to get suspect #1 to betray suspect #2, the detectives will often emphasize the length of the jail time suspect #2 will receive. While suspect #1 might emphasize his loyalty to suspect #2, the detectives know that if suspect #2's ability to "police" disloyalty goes away, so will much of the loyalty.

Sorry, We're Selfish

"I am willing to die for four uncles or eight cousins."
—J. B. S. HALDANE, biologist

Everyone on this planet is alive today only because all of their ancestors, in an unbroken chain over millions of years, managed to survive long enough to reproduce. If selfishness is part of our nature, it's because the genes for selflessness often didn't make it on to the next generation.

But despite our innate selfishness we've found ways to cooperate, if only because cooperation is so valuable a tool. We cooperate, as we have seen, because our social institutions preach the value of cooperation, and, more importantly, because we watch each other like hawks. Over the course of our evolution we learned to police each other's behavior.

This, perhaps, addresses one of the questions we raised earlier: why do we need police? We need police because, as optimal as it might be for the race as a whole, there was no evolutionary path that led to full cooperation. There is too much benefit to cheating, to being a freeloader, and so cheaters and freeloaders will always be with us, and will be a part of each of us as well.

So does this mean that animals can never be altruistic? What about the mother lion defending her cub? What about the honeybee whose decision to sting an intruder leads to her death?

Sad to say, cases of altruism in the animal kingdom are actually fairly rare and almost always turn out to be consistent with the rule of maximizing the success of one's genes. A mother lion will defend her cubs against great risk because each of those cubs has half of her genes; three of these cubs combined have more of her genes that she does! Less direct relatives, cousins and uncles, share smaller portions of our genes, but enough for it to make sense to take some risks for their sake, as noted in Haldane's somewhat ironic quote above.

There are some populations of animals, such as honeybees, in which most of the population sacrifices itself willingly (sort of) for the good of the queen. In these societies the worker bees cannot reproduce; the queen releases a hormone that prevents it. Because of the unusual genetics of these insects, the worker bees share three-fourths of their genes with the queen, which is usually more than they share with each other. So, lacking opportunities to breed themselves, their best chances of having their genes survive is to support the queen. Interestingly, when worker bees manage to avoid the queen's hormone and reproduce, their offspring is killed by their fellow workers. The workers support the queen because they are more closely related to the queen than they are to each other.

So, I regret to say, selfishness, not altruism, is the norm in the animal kingdom.

This brings us back to the question raised at the beginning of this essay: why are police willing to take on the risks and frustrations of police work? This question is compounded by what we've learned about evolutionary biology. Police bear the burden of "policing" good behavior; the rest of us are freeloaders.

When a member of a tribe of primitive men shouted for help, the rest of the tribe quickly rushed to help. It was understood that this was important to the survival of the entire tribe. But in our modern cities a woman cries for help and is ignored. If she is lucky, someone will call the police. We have delegated the responsibility for our common safety to the police. Police officers, like everyone else, evolved to have a strong sense of fairness and a quick eye to spot when they are being cheated. So why do they agree to take on the job, letting the rest of us freeload?

There is no definitive answer to these questions, but here are three "just-so stories" for your consideration.

Theory #1: Status

In primitive times, there were no formal police, but there was bad behavior. And surely there were some individuals, tougher and less risk-averse than their peers, who served as "primitive police," helping to enforce the rules. These primitive police supported their tribal chief, and no doubt were first in line to become chief when the chief died. These primitive police probably helped define the rules, as well as enforce them. This was certainly a high-status role, with favored access to food, luxuries and mates.

Those with the physical and behavioral attributes to play this role did well, and their genes prospered. But society has changed. Police work is no longer high-status, but our genes don't know that. The tendency to want to play the policeman role is still with us, even if the rewards of this role have evaporated.

One data point that supports this theory is the ongoing struggles in police departments in dealing with "dirty cops" who take bribes or otherwise benefit from their close association with the criminal element. Perhaps this difficulty stems from the genetic legacy of the primitive policemen, who were accustomed to having high status in society, and having a role in making the rules, not just enforcing them.

Theory #2: Violence

Maybe I've watched Sipowicz give one too many tune-ups, but it seems to me that police live a lot closer to violence than most of us. If *NYPD Blue* is any guide, police are comfortable with violence, and even take a certain adrenaline pleasure in violent situations.

Primitive man was much closer to violence than we are, and no doubt comfortable with violence; even taking pleasure in handing it out was rewarded. The genes for violence prospered. But in today's society, an individual with a tendency toward violence has very few acceptable outlets once he reaches adulthood. A job on the force may be the best of several poor options for someone who needs a certain amount of physical violence in his life.

One data point that supports this theory is the ongoing problem police departments have with unauthorized violence. This suggests that some on the force feel the need—or the desire—to use violence more frequently than the rest of society deems appropriate.

Theory #3: Transcendence

If we accept that genes drive much of our behavior, then one of the behaviors that our genes created was the ability to think, to reason, to plan: we became intelligent and self-aware. We get to make conscious choices, in ways that alligators and honeybees do not. As we have seen, man evolved with a strong sense of fairness. Perhaps some of us, observing our society, have decided that we want to be part of standing between criminals and victims, between chaos and civilization. For these individuals, the unfairness, the dangers, the difficulties, are less important than the opportunity to play a role in being on the right side. Their commitment to fairness and justice overrides these other considerations.

Because we are all, after all, thinking beings. Evolution left us with an enormous smorgasbord of behavioral legacies, and one of these was the ability to reason and to make decisions that appeal to the best of these legacies, not the worst. We all have these choices, and some of us make better ones than others. For my money, the detectives of *NYPD Blue*, and the real-life police officers in our street, demonstrate the best of our evolutionary legacy, and have made a choice to go with the best of our natures. Like all the detectives on *NYPD Blue*, Sipowicz is on the job because, for all his gruffness, he cares about our fragile society and wants to help the weakest among us. True or not, this is the just-so story I like best.

Glenn Yeffeth is the editor of numerous books, including Taking the Red Pill: Science, Philosophy and Religion in *The Matrix. Eighty-three percent of his behavior is attributable to Darwinian factors, and most of the rest is due to a head injury suffered as a child.*

ROXANNE CONRAD

Extra Points for Strippers: The Existential Cop Show Scoring System

Is NYPD Blue the best police show ever made? Roxanne Conrad does the math for us.

"New York: the only city where people make radio requests like 'This is for Tina—I'm sorry I stabbed you.'"
—CAROL LEIFER

"New York is an exciting town where something is happening all the time, mostly unsolved."
—JOHNNY CARSON

FIRST OF ALL, let me make it clear: I love cop shows. Yep. From *Naked City* to *Dragnet*, from *Homicide: Life on the Street* to *Third Watch*, if the show's got a flatfoot, a plainclothes detective or even an *ex*-cop in it, I feel compelled to watch it at least a few times.

So, I have all this experience with TV law and order... and yes, before you ask, I watch those shows too. You know, *Law & Order Classic*, *Law & Order: The Next Generation*, *Law & Order: SUV* (protecting urban Humvee owners everywhere) and of course, *Law & Order: CIA*. Or am I getting it mixed up with some other acronyms? NCIS? CSI? CYA?

Ahem.

What surprised me, when I first began watching vintage black-and-white cop shows—like the aforementioned *Naked City*, *Dragnet* and even *Highway Patrol*—I found there are elements that simply never change. And if they do change, they signal a dramatic rise in the cheese factor of the show...take away the grit and grime, and you automatically lose some of the *gravitas*. Think about *Homicide: Life on the Street* (surely one of the grittiest shows ever) versus, oh, *Silk Stalkings*. In *Homicide*, nothing matched. The walls were industrial blah. The only time they ever changed the furniture was when someone died on it. *Silk Stalkings* had neon *inside* the police station. Unlike science fiction, in which gritty, secondhand sets mostly signal gritty, crappy budgets (*Firefly* notwithstanding), the finest cop shows want to strip away the fancy doodads to focus you right on what's important.

Like sex, strippers and booze.

So join me in a totally biased, entirely unscientific assessment of our favorite precinct, the 15th.

The Utterly Biased, Unscientific Scoring Scale

100%	So gritty and realistic it should be arrested for impersonating an officer
80%	Dennis Franz buys it a drink
60%	Cagney & Lacey interrogate it, but let it walk
40%	The cops from *Barney Miller* feel superior
20%	Even Chris & Rita from *Silk Stalkings* snicker
0%	Not even the dumbest stupid criminals would tremble

Setting: 100%

Sure, you can set a cop show anywhere. Heck, you can set 'em in space (*Starcops*, *Outland*). There are, of necessity, police in nearly every place on Earth; if there are more than five people in one place, odds are one of them will be a hooker and one will be a cop. Or act like one, anyway.

But in achieving a high score in *this* system, your setting needs to have grit. It's got to be down and dirty. It's got to have mean streets, teeming masses, crazy people, history and—most of all—garbage. Garbage is essential for a good cop show.... How else do you tackle the bad guys? Doing it on concrete hurts. The best garbage tackles weren't actually done in *NYPD Blue*, though another Stephen Bochco show has the honor. The ear-chewing Detective Belker of *Hill Street Blues* performed flying, snarling tackles into trash with the greatest of panache. He's the man to beat, if he doesn't beat you senseless first.

Back to our city recap:

Naked City: New York City.

Hill Street Blues: New York City.

Law & Order, including variations: New York City.

Streets of San Francisco: Er, San Francisco. But Karl Malden looked menacing enough to make up for it.

Miami Vice:...Miami probably does have mean streets, but there's a lot of neon, and there were pastel jackets and Don Johnson involved. I'm just sayin.' (However, they had Jai-Alai and Helena Bonham Carter before it was cool.)

If there's neon glowing in *NYPD Blue*, it's dirty, flickering and spelling out the name of a beer you wouldn't dare drink. Their New York City is even meaner than the streets patrolled by *Third Watch*...okay, it's the same streets, but somehow, the 15th Precinct looks scarier.

Nobody on *Blue* lives in a fancy apartment—unless he's a victim or a criminal—and the apartments look authentically cramped and multi-generational. Furniture is haphazard. In fact, the fanciest thing I've ever seen in any cop's apartment so far is Sipowicz's glorious tropical fish tank.

Heck, I wouldn't dare go and be a skel there. Donna Abbandando could kick my ass, let alone Sipowicz.

Full marks.

Drinking: 100%

All good cops must consume alcohol.

This is a rule, not a guideline. If you're a teetotaling police officer, you'd damn well better show off your ninety-days-sober AA chip when you announce you're turning down a beer.

Cops go to bars. They go there a lot. (Sure, you never saw Joe Friday slamming back boilermakers back in the *Dragnet* days, but I just assume it happened off-camera.) When an emotional crisis comes, you're sure to either end up on the barstool sucking down firewater or staring moodily at a full glass you can't drink because you've been clean and sober for nearly a year since the last time you fell off the wagon, slugged your boss, hired a hooker and woke up rolled in an alley with your service weapon missing and later found at the scene of a murder.

(Oh, come on, you're saying it doesn't happen? Andy Sipowicz, the quintessential cop's cop, slugs his boss, moodily eyes liquor, gets drunk, gets rolled and is implicated in murder all the damn time. It's character-building. Not to mention Emmy-winning.)

NYPD Blue is clearly the show to beat on this breathalyzer test. First of all: well, Andy. I mean, case closed. In the *pilot* he was drunk and doing the horizontal mambo when he got shot. That takes a phenomenal appreciation of this hard-and-fast cop rule. Second example: Det. Diane Russell. Before we were through the second season, Andy was busy mother henning Diane to cope with her drinking problem. Andy, naturally, had relapses, principally in season three, when he returned to hit the bottle under the stresses of new fatherhood and sweeps weeks. Diane seemed to relapse whenever someone said the word "bar." She dipped in and out of sobriety so often that, by the time she relapsed again in season eleven's "Keeping Abreast," I'm surprised Andy didn't just give in, pull up a barstool and join her. I would have.

Total points: Andy lectured about sobriety a lot, which just points out how much of a problem there was, so I give them the full ride.

Drugs: 80%

It's imperative to have regular drug messages in cop shows. It's the Thing To Do. Usually this is accomplished by busting the dealers or skels, or possibly by busting the white-collar slick in the middle of his business meeting and leading him away in handcuffs as his crisply-pressed flunkies gape in horror. (This is a staple of *Law & Order*, of course.)

But in the *really* good cop shows, we have all this *plus* the Old Friend scenario.

Note that there are really two Old Friend scenarios.... One happens when the Old Friend is suspected of a murder that he couldn't have committed because, well, he's our *Old Friend*. Only, naturally, he did do it and he gives us that cold-blooded smile as he explains exactly how he duped us, and by the way, double jeopardy attaches.

This is the other one, though. It goes like this: an Old Friend shows up and needs help/money/advice. Sooner or later, we discover he's popping pills/shooting up/having sex for crack. Eventually, we use valuable prime-time minutes to dry out said Old Friend and set him on the straight and narrow, only to have him tragically die because the dope was just too powerful. Plus, we get to sit at the bar and moodily eye the glass of whisky we can't drink because of the ninety-day sobriety chip.

Kathy Bates directed a terrific example of this in season three called "I

Love Lucy," except the Old Friend didn't die (which sometimes happens if it isn't sweeps week and Andy isn't falling off the wagon).

Even more powerfully, we can have one of the regular cast members go through the Heartbreak of Addiction, tenderly nursed by his comrades (but in a manly way, dammit).... However, in this case, you only get points if the addiction causes the regular cast member to confess buried secrets, have wild monkey sex with someone inappropriate or go into a coma for the rest of the season. The best example of this falls not within *NYPD Blue*, but *Third Watch*. Technically, it wasn't drugs, but a *serious* drinking problem for Officer John Sullivan, but hey, we still got rambling delirium and the whole shebang. Or, alternatively, the granddaddy of buddy cop shows: *Starsky and Hutch*. Remember when Hutch got hooked on smack, 'cause the bad guys kept him prisoner and leered at him evilly while giving him regular injections, and Starsky had to manfully and tenderly care for him during cold-turkey rehab? Oh, yeah. That episode alone explains the wealth of speculation about the nature of the S&H relationship.

NYPD Blue score: Because none of the main characters has succumbed to the Evil Lure of Drugs, I have to grade them down to a solid 80%. Although they've all succumbed to the evil lure of *something*. And speaking of that....

Sex: 100%

Oh, come on. It's not called *Blue* for nothing, is it? Sex is the engine that revs the show. Back in the *Naked City* days (the name not withstanding) sex was something proposed in the shadows by a writer who was whacked by the censors before anybody got wise. Girlfriends and wives were acceptable. Sex really wasn't.

By the time *NYPD Blue* rolled around, cable was starting to kick network hiney, which still couldn't be shown on the air. Skinemax...er, Cinemax...was baring body parts right and left. Workplace romance had always been a big staple of cop shows, ever since Angie Dickinson brought her sexy-but-unobtainable *Police Woman* into America's living rooms. (And who can forget the immortal *Silk Stalkings*?) Still, the more straitlaced cop shows weren't into baring skin, unless it was dead and in the morgue.

The cops on *NYPD Blue*, on the other hand, didn't just have flings, they had torrid romances, crushes, spats and occasionally fellatio in the interrogation room. Sometimes they were too busy having personal lives to catch the crooks, just like the rest of us. And don't forget, this cop show gave us the ever-famous "buttwatch".... Whose would be bared during sweeps *this* season?

Gotta give them the full score for that alone.

Pregnancy and Loss of Same: 60%

First there's the sex, then there's the complications.

Every decent cop show in which a female cop is having sex will eventually have her announce those dreaded words, "I'm late." And she doesn't mean for a lunch date at Spago, either. Inevitably, for dramatic effect, those nearly infallible birth control products end up being cause for litigation.

Why is this necessary? Because nice as it is to have Resolved Sexual Tension (RST) as opposed to Unresolved Sexual Tension (UST), the truth is, people happily having sex like bunnies turns out not to be very dramatically interesting. Inevitably, we have to screw around with it. No pun intended.

Because then we get the inevitable Male Cop Angst, which revolves around men being protective of their pregnant but still-kick-ass girl-friends/wives. Case in point: Diane and Bobby Simone. By season five's "Sheedy Dealings" Diane is pregnant, and just a few episodes later "You're Under A Rasta" trotted out the inevitable Bobby/Diane fight about working—and getting shot at—while pregnant. In traditional cop show fashion, the issue was resolved, but ridden hard for its dramatic potential, when Diane lost the baby three episodes later. It wasn't the last (or even the first) storyline about sex, pregnancy and babies, but it was certainly the most true to form.

Later on, of course, we had the necessary variant of this theory: the foster child. Fancy had one, who came back in a variation of the Old Friend drug story. Currently, Baldwin has one, with the necessary load of horrendous personal history. (And, soon, drug problems. Betcha.) Sipowicz and main squeeze Connie McDowell have her sister's orphaned baby to care for...and you know why the baby's orphaned, right? That's right. Drugs/alcohol/abuse.

NYPD Blue gets a good 60%. It'd get more, except really, most of their pregnancies end up coming to term, and then we get into the com-plications of Child Care, which is not as dramatically interesting. The Trauma of Birth episode is always good for flop sweats, though.

Shooting People: 80%

If you're a New York City cop, you have to not only shoot people with a fair amount of frequency, you also will be required to shoot them under suspicious circumstances. There will be an IAB investigation. You will be required to turn over your shield and piece, but you'll do it resentfully, jaw muscles fluttering, as if you don't actually understand that this is part of the dramatic process for a character arc in Cop Land. (Hey, good movie, by the way. Who knew Sly Stallone could pull it off? And bonus points to a manic Ray Liotta for screaming, "Being right is not a bulletproof vest, Freddy!")

I won't even bother with the litany, but even Lt. Tony Rodriguez recently underwent a shellacking from the Rat Squad, and he didn't even *shoot* the crazy bastard who shot him. Although I suppose in a cop-shoots-cop-shoots-cop scenario, everybody's wrong eventually. (I did like *Third Watch's* marvelous John Woo-like shootout at the end of the 2003 season, with Yokas, Cruz and that lovable lug Boscarelli blazing away at each other. Mysteriously, no one's off The Job. They're a lot more lenient across town, apparently.)

Shooting people happens with such regularity that I'd have to grudgingly award them 80%. I'm holding off of the 100% because I'm waiting for PAA "Gay John" Irvin to pull out a .45 and take down a mugger while he's off duty.

Getting Shot: 40%

Sipowicz got shot in the pilot. People get winged, wounded and generally scared out of their minds on a fairly regular basis, but actually, *NYPD Blue* has been fairly leery of the get-shot-come-back-in-two-weeks-without-a-limp plot device. James Martinez got shot, and nearly lost the use of his legs; Sylvia Costas should have worn a flak vest to work at the courthouse. But since it's not one they use very often, I'm only giving them partial marks. Which brings me to . . . .

Dying: 100%

It's the ultimate sweeps stunt. Forget about eating bugs on *Fear Factor*; so far, at least, none of the reality shows have killed off a contestant (although it's early days, yet).

Happens all the time in police shows, though. "Cut down in a hail of gunfire" is always a very popular ending, although, surprisingly, not much used on *NYPD Blue....* It relies on the lingering deaths, generally.

So let's do the roll call of the fallen.

Bobby Simone. It was a real tearjerker of an end for this surprisingly powerful character arc, with stellar performances all around. Although Sipowicz had lost Det. John Kelly as a partner when David Caruso decided to swim with the movie sharks, he hadn't actually *buried* one before. And bonus points for making it a fatal illness, and one that wasn't the overworked Big C. From his first symptoms to the last rites, Bobby's slow descent was painful and effective.

Sylvia Costas. Technically only a cop-in-law, Sylvia still had an incredibly effective exit. Tragic, horrifying and another blow to the already overburdened Sipowicz, this one had real teeth. Although she died in a hail of bullets, it didn't feel contrived, and it gave PAA John Irvin the chance to demonstrate that being gay doesn't mean you don't have the courage of a lion.

Andy, Jr. Yes, another member of Clan Sipowicz joined the alumni club when he was—you guessed it—gunned down in a hail of bullets during a holdup. Another big *ouch* of an episode, which naturally parked Sipowicz on the bar stool, eyeing the glass of whiskey.

Danny Sorenson. The poster child for What Not To Do, Danny (the still-cherubic Rick Schroeder) started well and ended badly, going out in a haze of hookers, mobsters, bullets and drugs/alcohol. But he gets creative points for doing it off-screen, and we got a much-delayed grief when Danny's decomposed remains were uncovered at a dump site months later.

A bunch of ex-spouses are *really* ex.... Rita Ortiz's hubby, Tony Rodriguez's wife (which is convenient, since they're now making love together) and Bobby Simone's wife (but off-camera) all provided grist for the dramatic mill (and funeral home trade) during the run of the show.

So far, most recent Sipowicz partner John Clark, Jr., is hanging in there, but his dad, John "Dutch Boy" Clark, recently ate his gun after a nasty IAB incident, so the time-honored tradition continues.

Eating your gun is a tradition on its own, of course. If you're a cop, you're required to sit in the dark at least once with your .38 and a bottle of scotch, fingering your ninety-day sobriety chip and counting how much your pension is worth.

Score: the full ride.

Looking Like Real Cops (male)
or Like Real Fashion Models (male/female): 100%

Bless him, Dennis Franz just looks like a cop. That's probably not much comfort to him, after playing about twenty-nine various police and law enforcement roles in his career, but it's a huge strength.

He's not the only one. There's also Officer John Sullivan on *Third Watch*, who looks peeved at the world most of the time, and unapologetically like he never took a Pilates class in his life. And Karl Malden in *Streets of San Francisco* never worried about buffing up, either.

However, only *male* cops get this privilege. If you're a female TV cop, you'd better look damn good in your uniform (and be no larger than size four). Plain is *so* not done, unless you're visiting from another precinct. Skanky hos can look as rank as possible, but if you're on The Job, you'd better be buffed, coiffed and ready for the ShowerCam™.

One possible exception to this is the delightful Officer Faith Yokas on *Third Watch*, who is no fragile flower. I can see her kicking her partner's ass, and most of the time, we'd pay to watch that happen.

Lately, though, having a glossily perfect male cop is also an *NYPD Blue* specialty. Out with Detective Martinez, in with Det. Baldwin Jones, who could take off his clothes for money at just about any La Bare club out there.

I give 'em a solid 100%: surly, hard-drinking, scruffy males; petite, perfectly tough females; and hunk o' burning love bonus points.

And speaking of La Bare . . . .

Strip Clubs: 80%

Now, everyone knows that to be in the running, *any* cop show must have scenes in a strip club. I don't care if it's *Kindergarten Cop*; at some point, there must be a woman onstage and wild-eyed men stuffing sweaty bills into her thong.

Every cop show has it. The question is, how *often* do they have it? The short-lived *Big Apple* of a few years back actually had a cop *undercover* in a strip bar. In *The Sopranos* (not technically a cop show, but definitely in the law-and-order category) Tony actually owns the joint, which gives us ample opportunity for totally gratuitous T&A.

On network TV—even *NYPD Blue*—the T is covered, and the A is generally in long focus, which seems to be the lingering difference between network and cable. However, in no fewer than *twenty-five* episodes, our intrepid detectives ventured into these dens of sin (or possibly hives of scum and villainy). Particularly noteworthy is that the stripper factor ratcheted way up high after Danny Sorenson joined the cast. In fact, obsession with a particular stripper ended up earning Danny that special resting place on the shore.

I'd give the show a solid 80%, mostly on the strength of Danny's performance in this area. However, none of the female detectives worked undercover in a strip club, which in cheesier shows would be bound to happen, so . . .

Life Imitating Art: 80%

Art imitates life. But sometimes, life begins to imitate art, which leads to a giant whirligig of fun, as Xander Harris of *Buffy The Vampire Slayer* would say. *Buffy* was, in fact, one of the most noticeable leaders in this field, in that it popularized all kinds of language that existed nowhere but the Joss-Whedon-verse, such as "getting a wiggins." As in, "I'm getting a wiggins about this subject."

NYPD Blue definitely earns its points. "Lawyered up" is a phrase that became instantly recognizable and useful, even inside the law enforcement community. In a time when "breaking balls" was preferred by the cops in the know, sadly it was not censor-friendly. Instead, the writers coined the phrase "squeeze their shoes," which sufficed nicely until the eighth season, when the censors seemed to hit the bottle and curled up in the corner, weeping. That was when phrases like "I'm gonna break balls on this one!" just went sailing right over the plate.

"He's going to flip" no longer portends acrobatics; it means one skel ratting on another. And everybody knows what a skel is now, too.

Just the other day I heard that an accountant across the hall was going to "reach out" to his friend in Accounts Payable because he "had juice" and could "get them out of a jackpot."

However, the next time my boss comes in to "tune me up," I think I'm gonna have to get a load on first.

Score: Oh, heck, give them 80% out of 100. They get a twenty- percentage-point handicap because, well, they're not *Buffy*.

What? I never said I had to score fairly.

Bonus Points: Strange Plots
(courtesy of the marvelous episode guide at TV Tome—www. tvtome.com)—All together, worth an additional 20% of weird, offbeat, creamy goodness.

Medavoy and Martinez work a strangulation murder case that appears to be the work of a cross-dresser. Andy has a bad tooth, hates needles and tries to prevent a dentist from jumping off a twenty-eighth floor ledge; he fails.—season one, "Jumpin' Jack Fleishman"

I ask you, what can you say to that?

Medavoy changes to a high-fiber diet.—season two, "The Final Assignment"

Once again, the show was ahead of its time. Note that in season five, Sipowicz was already taking Viagra. However, I'm glad they didn't save this one for sweeps.

Medavoy's neighbor is the victim of a fortuneteller's scam; the resulting curse gives him a rash.—season two, "Don We Now Our Gay Apparel"

I want to know what they were drinking when they pitched that idea. I couldn't really give them points, but it does deserve a big raised eyebrow.

Lesniak and Martinez's case involves a con artist who sells a black box to homely women, promising them beautiful skin.—season two, "Large Mouth Bass"

Never mind what they were drinking, I want to know what they were smoking, because it sounds like a *Buffy* plot that got lost on the way to Mutant Enemy.

Andy and Bobby travel upstate when a potential suspect is caught there, Bobby uses the trip as a chance to let his pigeons get a workout.—season two, "Travels With Andy"

Now I have an eerie vision of pigeons doing step aerobics. Not good.

Simone and Sipowicz investigate the murder of a Puerto Rican teen because he used to make some paintings in Little Italy.—season two, "UnAmerican Graffiti"

I ask you, what better reason could there possibly be? Everybody's a critic.

A terminally ill infant helps the detectives locate a serial rapist.—season two, "The Bank Dick"

Too many jokes, and none of them are remotely tasteful.

Russell and Lesniak work a case involving a man who was left to die of a drug overdose; that leads to a chance to nail a fence.—season three, "Curt Russell"

I don't know about you, but I just had the weirdest carpentry moment.

Donna's hairdresser has a problem with her ex-boyfriend wanting to hijack the truck of her current boyfriend.—season three, "We Was Robbed"

Oy. I'm so tired of that clichéd old plot device.

The ex-girlfriend's father is also on the scene and suffering from the electric shock he received while trying to use an electric chain saw in the bathtub.—season five, "I Don't Wanna Dye"

...But not as tired as I am of this one. Didn't they do this on *Touched By An Angel?* But damn, I love that they did it with a straight face.

So let's recap. Each category is worth ten points, for a total of 110:

Setting:	10
Drinking:	10
Drugs:	8
Sex:	10
Pregnancy and Loss of Same:	6
Shooting People:	8
Getting Shot	4
Dying:	10
Looking Like Real Cops (male) or Like Real Fashion Models (male/female):	10
Strip Clubs:	8
Life Imitating Art:	8
Strange Plots: Bonus	2
Total *NYPD Blue* score:	94 out of 110

Nobody else even comes close.

To beat this record, you'd need to construct a cop show, set in New York City in a condemned police station too run-down to afford lights or bullets, in which everyone in the station has a terminal disease, a drug addition, an alcohol problem and/or is having a fling on the side with a coworker. Everyone would have to get shot *at* every episode, and get hit at least once a season. Half would have to die outright of their wounds. Half of the rest would have to expire artily in the hospital of exotic diseases, sparking a drug and drinking binge among the survivors. They'd invent an entirely new language consisting of profanity and slang, and most of the shows would take place in strip clubs or nudist camps.

And occasionally, they'd fight crime.

...nah. Even then, *NYPD Blue* still wins.

SOURCES: TV Tome (www.tvtome.com), *NYPD Blue* episode guides by Dennis Kytasaari. *The NYPD Blue* Lexicon (http://website.lineone. net/~rmeeks/)

Roxanne's novels include Stormriders, The Undead, Red Angel, Cold Kiss *and* Slow Burn *(as Roxanne Longstreet), and* Copper Moon, Bridge of Shadows *and* Exile, Texas *(as Roxanne Conrad). Her most recent work (as Rachel Caine) is the Weather Warden series, which includes* Ill Wind, Heat Stroke *and* Chill Factor, *with three more to come in 2005/2006. She also recently published (as Julie Fortune) an official* Stargate SG-1 *novel,* Sacrifice Moon. *Her short fiction has been featured in numerous magazines and anthologies. She confesses to an unnatural love of television, which includes an addiction to police dramas of all types. Visit her Web sites at www.artistsinresidence.com/rlc and www.rachelcaine.com.*